Running

Life Matters

MW00353114

Running

Life Matters

A Celebration of Running and Life Connections

RICHARD GOODWIN SR.

Mention of specific companies, organizations, people, or authorities in this book does not imply endorsement by the author or publisher, nor does mention of specific companies, organizations, people, or authorities imply that they endorse this book, its author, or the publisher. The information in this book is meant to supplement, not replace proper exercise training. All forms of exercise, including running, pose some inherent risks. As with all exercise, running, food and drink sampling, and dietary programs, you should get your doctor's approval before beginning or attempting.

Copyright © 2019 by Richard Goodwin Sr.

All rights reserved. No part of this book may be reproduced or transmitted in any form or by any means, electronic or mechanical, including photocopying, recording, or any information storage and retrieval system, without permission in writing from the author.

ISBN: 978-1-7338429-0-7 - Paperback
eISBN: 978-1-7338429-1-4 - ePub
eISBN: 978-1-7338429-2-1 - mobi

Printed in the United States of America   1 1 1 5 1 9

⊗This paper meets the requirements of ANSI/NISO Z39.48-1992 (Permanence of Paper)

Cover art and illustration by Richard Goodwin Jr.

CONTENTS

PREFACE

"We are what we repeatedly do. Excellence, then, is not an act, but a habit."

—Will Durant

When all is said and done, I guess it's fair to say there are probably as many different running styles as there are runners. Truly, no two running styles are identical! Running is a physical form of expression and, universally, runners love to express themselves however, wherever, and whenever they run. Running means different things to different people but at its essence, I think running's attraction is how it satisfies something in our primitive and core nature. It's the runner and the road, and all that's needed are some basic running clothes and running shoes (or not!) along with the motivation to make it happen. Once movement is unleashed, the rest takes care of itself—including affirmation of effort, insight, satisfaction, and the good health that follows. After additional time and repetition, running can become a natural and vital life component.

Like relationships or friendships we make, I think we similarly establish a relationship with the running process and running itself when we decide to run. That initial commitment and relationship can be basic or superficial at first because we're just starting out and scratching the surface about what running is and what it means to run and be a runner. But, over time we discover more about how running fits us and our lives, and how meaningful that running relationship becomes hinges somewhat on how we get along—how compatible we become. Running can, in some cases, truly become a partner and for some, a lifelong partner as a result of many years devoted to running. The more of ourselves we give to running, the more running will give us in return. And, like human relationships, the relationship we make with running can be full of ups and downs, doubt, insecurity, love, energy and fatigue, fulfillment, hope, promise, euphoria, disappointment, despair, pain—even suffering—and at times we can sometimes feel downright demoralized or even defeated. All in all, I've come to realize running is truly our friend and ally and that over time we learn to accept the ups, downs, and unpredictability connected with running. I don't believe we control running or that running controls us, nor do I think that should ever become a goal or objective. I think it's more a shared or symbiotic relationship with a mutually beneficial foundation built on give and take, mutual respect, understanding, tolerance, truth, and trust. And, isn't that, after all, the most promising and potentially healthiest and long-lasting relationship of all?

I think you will find this isn't a book that focuses mainly on how to run, per se, and it isn't primarily a technical account about the many varied and related aspects of running mechanics. Lots has already been written and said about those aspects of running by many, many running experts, nutritionists, doctors, and coaches. Nor is this book the result of some massive, scientific runner and running survey. No, this book is largely a compilation of thought and insight about running provided by yours truly and a small, select group of runners—from some accomplished lifelong runners, teacher colleagues, and friends I've known over the years. Writing this book has truly been a labor of love, and it reflects a lifelong love of running.

This is how it started . . .

INTRODUCTION

"Running eventually becomes less about time and performance; it becomes more about life."
                              —Richard C. Goodwin

On a spring afternoon several years ago, I was circling my nearby high school outdoor track on a weekend run, and an unexpected thought came to me: *Why not write a book about running and my running experiences?* But then I thought, *What to write?* I realized pretty much everything runners and others want to know about running had been written or said already.

After returning home, showering, and thinking more about writing a book on running, I began reminiscing about my running experiences, and recalled I'd run fairly consistently since 1978, having completed my first full marathon at age thirty-two—the Long Island Marathon—in 1981. Then, I began adding the many miles I'd run on this outdoor track over the years (after reviewing my runner logs), and came to the surprising realization I'd covered a distance approximating going from Atlanta to San Diego and back more than three times (well over ten thousand miles)—quite a number of quarter-mile laps! More importantly, I also remembered that while running those many laps around the track I'd been able to work through many concerns and solve lots of problems. I'd gained valuable life insight, and a deeper sense of spirituality and appreciation for the world and the people around me. I learned more about patience, understanding, and forgiveness, enjoyed the sights and sounds of wildlife, human life, improved my fitness, speed, and endurance, and became a more experienced, rounded, and complete runner. I also began to wonder more about what running means, or has meant to my various runner friends and colleagues, especially those who truly love running and have become lifelong runners.

So, after decades of running, being around other runners and the running community, I thought, *Why not sit down and offer some of the more memorable collective thoughts, insights, and running experiences that have come my way through running?* I also decided to reach out to that select group of accomplished runners I've known over the years and ask them to share their thoughts, insights, perspectives, and running stories. They have, and here they are!

Here are the runners, and here are their stories and thoughts about running. I have found their stories and insights unique, very special, impactful, and interesting, and I hope you will, too. Whether you are a veteran runner, new to running, or just thinking about running, I hope you'll enjoy what we now share with you. I also hope your journey in running and your running life will prove to be as textured, colorful, musical, full of light, and rewarding as ours has been!

> *"What lies behind you and what lies in front of you pales in comparison to what lies inside of you."*
> **—Ralph Waldo Emerson**

THE ATLANTA, GEORGIA, AJC PEACHTREE ROAD RACE

What is running about, and why do people run? The AJC Peachtree Road Race may provide some of the answers. The AJC Peachtree Road Race is a tradition in Atlanta. The year 2019 marked the fiftieth anniversary for the running of this most popular 10K event. It's grown in the number of participants to close to sixty thousand, and is known as the world's largest. It's a magnificent accomplishment by all involved from start to finish.

If you've ever wondered what it feels like to truly be part of a community of runners, just run the Peachtree and you'll readily see. So many people from so many different backgrounds come together on July 4 each year to celebrate our country's anniversary, running, and the fellowship of being runners with a challenging run on Peachtree Street, including the challenging uphill stretch of road known as "Cardiac Hill."

The wheelchair competition begins early and first, followed by elite, fastest runners and the "A" group of runners. Then, in successive waves of less speedy runners, starts become staggered in at five-minute intervals from the next fastest "B" running group, to "C," then "D," and so on to the final wave of runners. As each waiting group of runners is summoned to move forward to their start position, they are welcomed by an enthusiastic master of ceremonies, music, and a huge American flag waving high above and near the start line. After the singing of the national anthem and a few words of encouragement and praise (usually from Atlanta's mayor), there's the countdown, and the current wave of runners is released to begin the journey from the Lenox Mall location to the finish at Piedmont Park.

The author and son, Rich Jr., at the AJC Peachtree Road Race

Piedmont Park is grassy, open, and spacious, and is a most welcome sight for runners who have completed the race. I can say from experience it's not easy getting to the race and then returning home from the race, mostly because of the sheer mass of runners and spectators, but when you do arrive to the start line, and when you give it your best and finish this most challenging race, you truly appreciate what running is all about and the effort runners give. It's a struggle, for sure!

Weather for this Atlanta race is somewhat predictable, because temperatures are usually warm to hot with humid conditions. It can be rainy and even stormy, and scaling "Cardiac Hill" requires extraordinary effort. But, you get so much in return. Runners overcome. Mutual inspiration is the name of the game, and there's a keen sense of fellowship, family, community, and sharing. When you finally cross the finish line, have your picture taken, and move into Piedmont Park, you are given the official, colorful AJC Peachtree Road Race T-shirt. In this race, the shirt is earned and only given to race finishers. Runners cherish the shirt, and it becomes a runner's keepsake to wear proudly around town later that day and elsewhere for years to come! And, each year's shirt is always different and uniquely designed.

The Greater Atlanta community, along with the Atlanta Track Club and the thousands of volunteers, runners, and spectators, do an amazing job with each and every aspect of this race year after year. Let's just say runners who do the Peachtree will most certainly gain a new and life-lasting perspective about running, and what running means to them and the thousands of others surrounding them!

"What we think, we become."

—**Buddha**

Photo of 2013–2018 AJC Peachtree Road Race shirts

HOW I BECAME A RUNNER

by Bill Rodgers

I became a runner in 1963 with my older brother, Charlie, and our best friend, Jason. We ran cross-country, the king of sports! We made friends with this sport of road racing and marathon running, and it's been for a lifetime!

Early Recollections of Running

I remember running from home plate to first base. That's when, at age five, I connected running with speed. I knew the faster I made it to first base, the better my chances were I'd be "safe!" For me, then, running was wrapped around and part of a sport. Over time, I saw that running was important in sports, and speed, consistency, and endurance mattered.

When I got to fourth grade, the gym teacher—the much older, white-haired Mr. Reed—told us to run to the town's bandstand and back, which was around three-eighths of a mile off in the distance, as fast as we could! Weather conditions didn't matter to Mr. Reed. He told us to run our fastest, rain or shine, and that's what I and the rest of our gym class did. I discovered I was pretty fast and usually came in first, second, or third place. I discovered I liked to run all-out and didn't mind returning (gasping for air) under Mr. Reed's watchful eye of approval. Mr. Reed kept track with his trusty stopwatch and told us how fast we ran. We all liked to know if we were improving, and Mr. Reed liked to see our improvement.

2018 photo of my "Hometown Bandstand"

Then, some years later (back in the 1960s), when I was a high school junior, our school held an interclass track meet. Boys from grades nine through twelve who were not track-team members competed, and I was picked to run the quarter-mile event. We had a cinder track, and I borrowed a track-team member's spikes to run in. The gun went off and so did I, not knowing what to expect. I'd never run the quarter-mile distance on our track full sprint, but nevertheless, I peeled out around the first curve and moved around toward the 220-yard mark when the guy in the lead—a very fast senior runner with legs and feet churning forward and flailing about—suddenly lost his footing, and then fell and slid along and over those nasty, sharp, black cinders.

Ouch!

I kept sprinting to and through the 220-yard mark, confident I would win because the leader and only real competitor was now down and sprawled out on the track behind me. I felt an easy victory was at hand, but I didn't let up or slow my pace.

Then, as I approached the near curve toward the finish line, my thighs seized up and started burning. Somehow, I found myself slowing, and it became impossible to maintain my pace and turnover rate.

Well, I struggled to the finish line totally exhausted, and did win with a time of 60.5 seconds. The track coach, who was watching and timing the race, praised me for my 100-percent effort. I was so relieved the race was over and amazed the quarter-mile distance took so much out of me.

It wasn't until I came home after military service, when the first running boom took hold, that I finally discovered the sport of running and running as a standalone activity. Now some forty years later, with my baseball, football, and basketball–playing days behind, I continue to love running for the pure joy it brings. I'm part of the world of running and wouldn't have it any other way. I invite you to also think about your first recollections of running.

THE RUNNERS' LUNCH

In the early 1990s, while a restauranteur in a prior life, I had the good fortune—as you will readily see—of being a host and cosponsor of a local 10K race, providing postrace food, drink, and friendly hospitality to runners. Weather-wise, it was an ideal day in Upstate New York for a morning run, and the race itself was scheduled to finish just before lunchtime.

Around noon, and after completing their 10K distance, runners began streaming in one by one, and then they started coming through the front door in bunches. And, to my delight, legendary runners and race participants Joan Benoit Samuelson, Bill Rodgers, and Frank Shorter came in, too! They had completed the race, and the plan was for them to come into the restaurant, have some refreshments, and mingle with runners for a short time. As proprietor, I was thrilled they came in and "graced" my restaurant with their legendary presences! As a runner, I was equally thrilled to be in their company and in the midst of arguably the most accomplished and influential American distance runners in history!

Well, there they were. I greeted Frank Shorter, welcomed him to my restaurant, offered him something to eat and drink, and he decided to pass on the food but opted for a cold beer instead. Bill Rodgers and Joan Benoit Samuelson had both food and drink, and they sat with me, my wife, and five-year-old son, and they were so gracious to spend some time with us and allow us to be part of their lives for an hour or so. They all were terrific guests—so down to earth, approachable, friendly, and warm—and they were even willing to have a few pictures taken with us. Frank Shorter posed with my son, Richard Jr., and Joan Benoit Samuelson and Bill Rodgers were photographed with my family and me, and to this day I cherish those memories and photographs.

Photos of Joan Benoit Samuelson and Bill Rodgers with the author, wife (Judy), and son (Rich Jr.), 1993: "The Runners' Lunch"

"The Runners' Lunch" postrace photo; Bill Rodgers with runners

Years later, I spoke to Bill Rodgers and Joan Benoit Samuelson again at the prerace expo of the twentieth anniversary and running of the Disney World Marathon. And, much to my surprise, they remembered being at my restaurant and meeting me after that 10K race. Amazing!

I recently wrote to Bill Rodgers and asked him if he'd sign some of those old photos taken of him with my family on that special 10K race day. He wrote back and said he would be happy to, so I sent the pictures to him, and he graciously signed them and mailed the autographed versions back to me. Needless to say, I was thrilled again, because he didn't have to do that, but he did!

Now, several of those pictures have been framed and are proudly displayed in my den. They serve as a wonderful reminder of how terrific he is and how rewarding it is to still be part of the greater running community. On one of the photos he wrote, "Let's run forever!" After reflecting on that motivational thought, I've decided not to stop running anytime soon.

Yes, let's hope all of us in the running community have many more miles to run, amazing people to meet, and special places to go before our running days are over.

"Perseverance is not a long race; it is many short races one after the other."

—**Walter Elliot**

THE MARATHON: AN OVERVIEW AND RUNNER PERSPECTIVE

"No amount of wealth or fame can run a marathon."
—Richard C. Goodwin

I've heard over fifteen million runners enter sanctioned races per year, and of those, approximately five-hundred thousand run marathons. So, I suppose it's probably fair to say there are many more than those fifteen million "official" runners; they are those additional people who run or jog for the fun of it, and just decide not to enter race events.

I think runners who enter races find the 5K distance and the 10K distance very popular, followed by the half marathon, full marathon, and other longer races in order of popularity. And, when you think of it, with all the training and time that's involved, it makes sense. The marathon distance isn't for most runners when you consider the amount of work and dedication involved.

In 1980, the vast majority of marathoners were men, and now women marathoners are approaching half the entire field of runners. For women and men alike, running a full marathon is the culmination of mileage buildup. It's a day-after-day, week-after-week, and month-after-month grind until the day of the race. The marathon race day is the "reward" day—the day runners "cash in" on their training and sacrifice, and finally get the chance to run the full, official 26.2 miles!

Photo of the author, first marathon, 1981

No question about it, completing a marathon requires discipline and endurance, commitment and consistency, and the capacity and ability to overcome pain and adversity through sheer determination, resiliency, and faith in oneself. It's knowing you've run the first five miles, then the next five miles, and so on up to twenty miles, and then being able to continue to run that last 10K to the finish line. Some have said the twenty-mile point and that last 10K portion are really where the marathon begins. Yes, running a marathon isn't for everybody. Yes, only a small portion of all runners complete full marathons, and fewer still complete multiple marathons in their lifetimes.

Running the marathon distance takes time and lots of patience. Some finish the 26.2 miles in five to six hours; others finish a bit faster; some can finish between three and four hours, but completing a full marathon in less than three hours is truly a remarkable accomplishment. Just consider the pace. To break three hours, a runner must average just under seven minutes per mile for the entire distance! It's daunting, isn't it?

Age usually matters, since most runners slow down the older they get. Then there's the weight factor. It's no accident elite distance runners weigh less and run faster than the rest of the field. Why? It's largely about physics and the work or effort it takes to move the body weight from point A to point B. It's considerably more difficult to move a body weight of 185 pounds or heavier 26.2 miles than it is to move, let's say, a 145-pound or lighter body weight over the same distance, no matter how prepared the heavier runner is. Just ask your physics teacher or professor! Surprisingly, over the years I've not seen a component for weight consideration and adjustment factored into full-marathon time results, calculations, and runner placement and performance. It's been about age and gender, not weight.

So, now let's move on and say runners are fit and ready to run the full marathon. Success is at hand, and goals are about to be achieved. Right?

Not so fast.

Lots can happen in the final weeks and days leading up to the marathon. Runners can sustain a last-minute injury. They can get sick or experience unexpected fatigue, or they can come down with a case of last-minute jitters. They can even have a few sleepless nights before the race, and let's also not forget about the weather! Runners can train in cool or cold weather for months leading up to marathon day, but can be surprised by seventy-five-degree temperatures or hotter when they toe it up on race day! Now, that's a tough one. And then there's the chance of heavy, sustained rain and blustery wind during the race. It's not much fun slogging along roads covered by several inches of water with drenched feet. Running shoes, socks, and feet just don't like having to run 26.2 miles when they're soaked with water. Trust me, they've told me so! Or, it can be much colder than anticipated. Try running a marathon in sleet and freezing rain.

I think you get the picture, and maybe some of you have endured those experiences. The marathon can sometimes turn out to be a battle, with the runner at war with both the distance and the weather come race day. Even when the runner "embraces" the weather elements and adversity on race day, it can prove brutal nevertheless. But, if things line up as hoped and planned for on race day—including the weather—runners can have the super-great marathon experience they expected and trained for.

So, why do people try to run marathons knowing they might experience multiple ups and downs along the way? I guess it depends on the runner, but for many, it is their biggest challenge and accomplishment ever! It's the overcoming of aches and pains, limitations, and making all things possible. It's mind over matter. It's the celebration of life. It's the joy of the marathon journey. It's primitive and simple in nature. It's being honest with oneself, and it's about being able to say, "I did it!"

I can say from experience, you learn from each and every marathon you run and from each marathon you complete. You learn to deal with and overcome various challenges, and you toughen mentally, physically, and emotionally. You find no two marathons

Author Rich Goodwin Sr. after 1982 New York City Marathon

Photo of the author, 2016 Kiawah Island Marathon

"Run the New York City Marathon and meet the rest of the world."

—Richard C. Goodwin

WHAT'S TOO HEAVY?

The vast majority of runners find themselves somewhere behind the race leaders, ranging from running just behind to being way behind, and that can amount to time differences of many minutes and even hours in marathon races. Top runners work hard. They are consistent in their training and race preparation, and as a result, they are usually successful on race day. They also keep their weight in check and try to carry fewer pounds around with them from start to finish. They know it's the smart thing to do, because it means less work for them to move from point A to point B. They burn calories more efficiently and usually can keep their core body temperature in range. Their body's cooling system works more efficiently. They feel lighter on their feet as they move, and so on.

Overweight and heavier runners just don't win races! So, it's no secret that how much a runner weighs makes a difference, and the question becomes, "How heavy is too heavy?"

I've heard and have read that a runner who carries ten extra, unnecessary pounds around on a 26.2-mile marathon run can expect to give up approximately ten extra minutes in time. Five excess pounds costs around five extra minutes, and so on. Though the results are less dramatic on shorter-distance races, the principle remains the same: When runners carry less excess body weight, it usually results in faster times with less overall effort, all things being equal.

Does this mean all runners should pile up weekly mileage to burn extra calories, lose weight, and seek a "perfect" daily diet? Does it mean runners should do whatever it takes to try to become skinny?

Certainly not!

It's obviously not possible or practical for the vast majority of runners to pile on extra daily miles along with extreme self-imposed dietary restrictions. What fun would that be for most runners? Running and eating just wouldn't be the same, or as enjoyable!

But, the principle idea here is hard to dispute. Less weight improves the possibility of running distances faster. Shedding unnecessary pounds improves the chances of becoming more competitive and being able to attain new personal records (PRs) with overall less effort. Tweaking one's mileage and diet could very well nudge running performance upward, as the necessary running effort decreases when the weight comes off. For many of us, that is a worthy and realistic goal, especially when we and our running performances seem to have plateaued.

The bottom line is, we are who we are. Our sizes, shapes, body builds, bone structures, and resulting weights are largely in our DNA. But, we can make the most of it—the way we're naturally made—and through some extra effort and sensible food-and-drink diet, we can shave off some unneeded weight and increase our speed and endurance so we and our performances are best when race day rolls around!

> *"It does not matter how slowly you go*
> *as long as you do not stop."*
>
> —Confucius

RUN YOUR OWN RACE

Having a running partner, a training partner, can be fun and can provide a boost. You may be able to share common running goals, a similar commitment to running, and gain another valuable point of view or perspective. Running is, by and large, a solitary activity. It's the runner and the road, and the runner with his or her thoughts. But, having another to share the pace and distance with can provide a most welcome lift. There's the opportunity to talk, share ideas, move in a similar rhythm, offer encouragement, challenge, and that running relationship can prove to be significant.

Running partners sometimes select common races to enter. They formulate a common race strategy and agree on pace, and they sometimes travel together to the race site, share meals, and so on. The bonding that takes place between running partners can even last a lifetime!

But, as I and others have learned from experience, when it comes to race day and the race itself, the best laid plans can go astray once the race begins. All that was agreed upon previously by running buddies might be tossed aside. One or both of the running partners can unexpectedly sprint ahead, never to be seen again, leaving no logical explanation as to why, leaving those behind bewildered and sometimes experiencing a sudden and keen sense of betrayal. The expectations of running a race together (particularly a distance event) may prove to be unrealistic once race adrenaline and emotion kick in.

I think it takes extraordinary self-control and unselfish commitment to run a distance race alongside your running partner from start to finish. I've lived and raced through that and know. Being left behind can cause confusion, upset, and misunderstanding, and it can sap valuable mental and emotional energy.

So, I think the long and short of it is, regardless of the race plan agreed upon by running partners, as well as the expectations about how the race will be run, things happen, and runners need to go about their individual business and run their own race. If it turns out the race goes as planned, great! But, that's not what usually happens, so runners should be able to race with their eyes open and with a singular determination to run, not allowing that form of interference. They need to expect the unexpected, adjust and adapt accordingly, and run and finish the race with their own best effort on their own unrestricted terms.

Remember, in the end, it boils down to the race being yours. So, be sure to run it your way!

> *"As your running capacity grows, your tolerance and respect for others will, too."*
> **—Richard C. Goodwin**

What about Running Shoes?

If there's one thing I've learned after decades of running, it's that running shoes matter! And, no matter what a running-shoes salesperson says, it's about your opinions, running needs, shoe comfort, and effectiveness that matter most. There's plenty of information out there on the web and in various running magazines that provide shoe descriptions and reviews to help you with your shoe choice and purchase decisions. Also, going directly to the shoe manufacturer's home page and finding shoe information is also helpful. Specifications are usually provided, and when you visit a running-shoe store to buy your shoes, you'll go in knowing some important information.

I'd been having some Achilles-tendon problems, and the shoe salesman recommended a shoe with a steeper heel-to-toe drop. I took his suggestion, and it worked! There turned out to be less stress on my aging, aching Achilles, and over time the injury healed. No more Achilles pain! He knew what he was talking about, and I'm so grateful he did!

However, on a different, unrelated occasion, I spoke to a shoe salesperson and was astounded to discover I knew more about the shoe specifications than the salesperson did. I learned that my preliminary shoe research and knowledge helped me make a more informed and, ultimately, correct shoe-purchase decision.

So, I think runners need to be on their toes, so to speak, and should guard against being pushed, cajoled, or persuaded into shoe-purchase decisions. Buy shoes only after you believe they are the right ones for you! Further, if you find after running in a new pair of running shoes they don't work for you, just return them to the store and find a different pair to your liking. And, don't be shy or afraid to return them! The better running-shoe stores offer full refunds or exchanges. Please don't hold onto them thinking you'll adjust to them over time, continue to run in them anyway, or continue to run in discomfort. If you do, a running injury may be right around the corner.

And, when you've identified a running-shoe store with knowledgeable and competent salespeople, reach out to them when it's time to buy your next new running shoes. They'll serve you and your running needs best, and you'll enjoy your running and running progress more because of that relationship and their expertise.

You can, of course, buy your shoes directly from the manufacturer online, bypassing the store and salesperson, and in doing so, even save a few dollars along the way, but to do that, you'll need to know your exact shoe size and be absolutely certain about the shoe model you're buying. Shoe sizes and sizing vary from shoe model and manufacturer to shoe model and manufacturer, but once you know what works for you, then go for it, if you like.

But, in saying that, shoe models, designs, and specs do often change from year to year, so please don't assume, for instance, the 2019 model will be the same as the newer 2020 or 2021 models. Just because the model numbers stay the same doesn't mean the shoes themselves will stay the same. In all probability, you'll find the design and engineering of the shoes different in different years. Again, even though one year's model works for you, it won't necessarily mean subsequent yearly models and versions will also meet your running needs. It's really not cool when you've been running in shoes that really work, only to find out that that model version has been discontinued or replaced with a newer, reengineered version made with new materials that don't meet your running needs any longer. That's happened to me, and when it does, I need to start all over again to try to identify an adequate replacement. There's no question, it can involve some unanticipated adjustment and readapting to a new and different shoe and shoe manufacturer.

So, my advice is to stock up on an extra pair or two of the running shoes you like, know, trust, and that work for you, so when they disappear off the running-store shelves or are reengineered, you'll have an extra pair of shoes to fall back on until you've had time to find that adequate shoe replacement. Timing is everything, and you don't want to find yourself high and dry without those proven shoes when needing to prepare for or run an important race. Being a week or two out from race day isn't the ideal time to be thrashing about and on the hunt for shoe replacements, so it's best to plan ahead and not get caught short.

WHAT TYPE OF RUNNER?

Do you prefer running distance races, or do you like shorter runs? Or, do you like to run a distance that falls somewhere in between? Maybe you like to vary your running distances and enjoy racing from 5K to the full-marathon distance, and possibly even beyond! I think it's fair to mention here that one size doesn't fit all runners. And, fortunately, there's a variety of races and distances available to meet the needs and preferences of most runners.

Usually, runners favor certain distances over others. And, it's fine to favor shorter distances over longer ones. Actually, most runners do. For one thing, running shorter usually provides an opportunity to run a faster sustained pace. That's fun! Running longer usually results in keeping a slower sustained pace, and that's okay, too. I used to think marathon running was the only way to go. Then I discovered half marathons could be fun, and yes, even 10Ks and 5Ks could be equally rewarding in their own unique ways.

A facet to consider when alternating running distances is to either ladder them up or down, and either way can prove beneficial. If you ladder up, you build into the marathon distance in a consistent and logical way. Most running plans use this conventional, incremental approach to marathon preparation. But, I've discovered significant physical and even psychological advantages can be had when you train for and run your marathon first, then systematically through the year reduce running race distances to 13.1 miles, 10K, and then 5K.

Why?

Because you've already trained for and completed the toughest part of your training when you fulfill your marathon commitment, and then dropping down to the half-marathon distance just seems relatively easy by comparison. The 10K seems even easier and the 5K easiest. You find yourself actually looking forward to running the shorter distances throughout the rest of your running year.

I know, it does seem a bit backward or counterintuitive, but oh, what a relief it is to go shorter throughout the remainder of your running period!

Also, running at times that work best is so important. Runs should be scheduled around daily demands whenever possible. Runners should obviously ask themselves if the weather makes a difference to them. Do they, for instance, prefer running in sunshine, on hotter days, cooler days, during certain seasons of the year, and so on? I suggest trying it all out to see what works best. I've found it's much easier to go from training in warmer weather to racing in cooler weather than it is to go from cooler to warmer. But, as I've already mentioned, you can plan a cooler seasonal race only to be surprised by an unseasonably warm or hot race day! The weather is always going to be the big unknown, and while runners can control most of their training activities, we know the weather can be a big surprise come race day.

Much has been written about periodization—or the way to plan, schedule, and train—for longer term, yearly races. Knowing the distances we like to run, the climate and weather we can usually expect and prefer running in, and the race events we are targeting will help determine the training we need to do, and when and where we'll do it. Knowing the kind of runner you are will help drive the entire process.

Running and New Places

We usually train in familiar places, right? We run on familiar roads, tracks, hills, trails, and sidewalks, but we can race near to home or decide to travel to new and unfamiliar places. That's the beauty of racing! We can take our trained runner body wherever we want to race, and that can be fun, educational, and exciting. Seeing new and unfamiliar places can add to the race experience. Being among runners and others from different states and countries can provide variety and enrichment.

I'm not saying racing near home isn't rewarding and fun. Of course, it is! But I've always found I walk away from a new race-city location with much more than a new race time. It's truly an eye-opener. It's a stretch and new challenge, and after doing it a few times I get the hang of it and can make new-site racing adjustments easier and easier.

Coming out from your comfort zone can be a real growing experience. Yes, new places can be amazing, and the unfamiliar can be good. Turning your destination race into a race minivacation might result in you returning home refreshed, confident, and even more accomplished. The combination of racing near home and racing away from home can help keep running fresh, new, and more interesting.

Now, I know it's unrealistic to think most runners can travel outside the country and race all over the world, for obvious and various reasons. But, maybe an occasional race in a new town, city, or state will work just fine.

"You are never too old to set another goal
or to dream a new dream."

—**Les Brown**

THE RUNNING-LIFE
RELATIONSHIP

Some believe running mirrors life, and life mirrors running. For example, making it to age sixty-five is an accomplishment when you consider the many twists and turns that come along year after year. And, living past sixty-five into the seventies, eighties, and beyond is truly remarkable.

It's similarly amazing to continue running into those later years of life. It's an accomplishment to run as we age and experience how our bodies adjust and adapt along the way. Running, like life, is a journey; it's a parallel journey where our running experiences follow along with our life experiences. I, and many other senior citizens, have found it can be even more fun and gratifying to continue to run and compete past age sixty-five. Many runners have found they like and love running more in later life than they did decades before.

For younger runners, with many running years ahead of them, life and the running journey are yet to be determined, and hopefully will be filled with promise, good health, prosperity, insight, and success.

> *"When the sun is shining I can do anything; no mountain is too high, no trouble too difficult to overcome."*
>
> **—Wilma Rudolph**

WHAT WILL BE YOUR OLYMPICS?

The Summer Olympic Games usually provide amazing performances by many athletes. The runners outdo themselves, and their Olympic journeys are incredible to witness. Only a handful of all runners will ever be Olympic runners. But, that doesn't mean we non-Olympians can't set challenging goals and strive to accomplish them.

For those with speed, endurance, durability, determination, runner intelligence, and miles under foot, maybe it's qualifying to run a major marathon. For those of us just starting out, maybe it's to train for that first 10K. For competitive runners, maybe it's to consistently finish in the top five or top ten in their race division. Your goals can be what you want to commit to, and you are free to select what your "Olympics" will be.

Maybe the medal earned and received after finishing won't be an Olympic medal, but it will be significant because it will reflect hard work, dedication, performance, and crossing the finish line. And, to finish the race, runners first need to start and then see it through to the end. That's the grit and no-quit attitude it takes, and that's how you'll reach each and every goal and objective attempted.

When setting your race goals, be sure they are realistic and they challenge you. Then, chart your course and write your training plan, or select a plan from a reputable source that fits your training needs. Work the plan while trying to maintain a healthy life balance. Complete the plan, and you'll position yourself for success on race day.

Good luck in your next "Olympics!"

What will be your Olympics? (Photo of various race finisher medals)

Beware the Naysayers!

I'm always on the alert for those who, let's just say, aren't the most supportive of my running and just don't get the point of running and competition. Many years ago, I ran with one of my good friends almost daily over a period of several years. One of his bosses was overweight, didn't exercise, sat most of the day, and questioned why my friend ran. The boss told him running outside actually was unhealthy because of air pollution. He tried to discourage my friend from running, but my friend continued to run anyway. He ran the New York City Marathon at age forty and put down a Boston Marathon qualifying time (a "gun time") of 3:09 and change—a terrific accomplishment, for sure!

Around that same time, I worked for a bank in Mount Vernon, New York, and with one exception, I was the only serious runner on the staff. For the most part, running and training for a marathon was rare. Many people viewed marathon training and running as excessive, foolish, and dangerous. This was at the beginning of the first initial running-boom period, when most people knew little about marathon training. It was common to hear, "Oh, that's too far!" or "Are you crazy?" or "You'll hurt yourself!" or "I could never do that!" or "I'm not a runner!" or "Running is so boring!" or "I'd *never* want to run a marathon!" or "I've never liked to run!" or "I don't like to get sweaty!" and on, and on, and on!

And you know what? I occasionally hear similar comments and sorts of things today when people find out about the running

I do. Not everyone has their "reactions tape" playing and their instant reflex defense mechanisms ready to spring forth, but I still continue to be amazed by nonrunners who are couch potatoes, and yet, for some unknown reason, present themselves as authorities on running.

However, more often than not, I'm now met with more and more encouragement from people concerning my running. And, I'm met with less discouragement about my marathon training and running, although I do hear an occasional "Now be careful and don't overdo it!" out of a genuine concern for my health and well-being. I do appreciate those thoughts, and yes, I do train for marathons and run marathons differently now that I'm over seventy. I do remind myself to run a hard and sensible race to finish in one piece in order to live another day!

I've learned to surround myself with fellow runners, family, friends, and colleagues who are positive, affirming people who support me and the sport of running, and who offer encouragement instead of providing perpetual worry and discouragement.

> *"Sometimes a run down a road can seem like a stroll through a park."*
>
> **—Richard C. Goodwin**

Making the Most of Your Surroundings

After running seriously and consistently for over forty years, I've observed, as in life, runners and people in general should try to make the most of their surroundings. There are as many different runner techniques, styles, looks, and so on as there are runners. How we run, what we do when we run, why we run, when we run, and how we look when we run are highly individualistic measures reflecting, I think, who we are, our preferences, core differences, and lifestyles.

Where we run, however, is a totally different element of running to consider. Yes, it would be terrific if we all could enjoy our daily runs on nature trails or park trails in cool, crisp, clean, and clear air, but the running reality is we can't, don't, and won't! I run most days in hot, humid, heavy air just outside Atlanta, and wow, do I appreciate and love an occasional vacation run in New England, especially out on Cape Cod in the spring and fall. I find running there to be so invigorating, and I've experienced occasions on the Cape when I felt like I could run forever. I've adapted and adjusted to the Southern climate and have learned to train accordingly. I make the most of my surroundings, accept the monotony of daily running on the same familiar asphalt, sidewalks, and tracks, and I've learned to be grateful for what's available to me.

Photo of a Cape Cod Rail Trail (CCRT) section near Brewster, Cape Cod

Photo of "Giant Rocking Chair" at Brewster Green Resort, Cape Cod, Massachusetts. Brewster Green is a great place to vacation and access various Cape Cod places, activities, and the scenic Cape Cod Rail Trail (CCRT) for running, walking, and biking.

How many of us live in Boulder, or Eugene, or other places where, as we've read or heard, "running nirvana" truly exists! If we're goal-oriented, love to run, and have accepted running as being part of who we really are, and running has been woven into our life and lifestyle, then we owe it to ourselves to make the most of running in our surroundings.

With that being said, I'm not suggesting we shouldn't explore new and different places to run. By all means, I think we should at least consider doing that whenever and however those opportunities present themselves to us. If we're feeling "stale" in our running routine and feel tired of running in our normal, home-running environment, maybe we should seek new and different places and running surroundings for a much needed, appreciated, and uplifting pick-me-up running experience elsewhere. Again, my place has become Cape Cod, and the times that work for me and my family are June and October. My wife and I travel there for a minivacation, I run, and we have some fun! When on the Cape, my ten days of running are factored into my training centered on one Cape Cod race I select to run. That two-week period, change in climate, and Cape Cod running routine make all the difference in the world, and I find I'm refreshed, eager, and ready to run the familiar home turf again when I return to the Atlanta area.

Alberto Salazar, 1982 Falmouth Road Race

Runners and spectators, 1984 Falmouth Road Race

The author at finish area of 1984 Falmouth Road Race

"Reach for it. Push yourself as far as you can."
—**Christa McAuliffe**

What Goes Up Should Come Down

Do you like running up hills? Or, do you prefer running down hills? Maybe you like running both up and down hills, but the runners I know just like a fairly flat course to race and accept hill training as part of their running regimen, knowing hill running helps with both speed and strength.

It can be daunting to run up a very steep hill in the middle or toward the end of a very hot-weather race, especially after fatigue has set in. Sometimes the race you run will be very hilly, and what I mean by that is the majority of the distance is either uphill or downhill with a few fairly level intervals along the race course. If you've trained on hills, you'll most likely handle them, but if not, you'll struggle. Know your course, study the race map, topography, and total elevation change, and you'll prepare mentally for what's ahead. Some shorter races and newer, smaller races may not furnish this information, but you can ask around to find out. Even consider driving the course ahead of time, if you can, so you'll have a solid visual of it. Knowing about and training for the hills is the best combination, so you'll not be surprised by the elevation changes and so you'll be able to efficiently and effectively navigate the hills you encounter.

I recently ran a charity 10K in a hilly area near my home and was surprised by the number and severity of the hills. It was very challenging, for sure, but I told myself over and over I would get through them and reminded myself, *What goes up must come down.* It made a big difference, and helped me conquer those hills and finish strong!

"I dwell in possibility."

—Emily Dickinson

More People Would Do It

When you think about it, wouldn't many more people be distance runners if it was easy? It takes an honest marathon effort to run marathons, and sitting on the couch watching TV just isn't going to get a person across the finish line at 26.2 miles. Talking about it isn't going to move the body 26.2 miles, either. Just thinking about running distances isn't enough to do it! Reading about running won't do it. Knowing someone who is a distance runner isn't the same as actually *being* a distance runner. Distance runners know it takes consistent training, sacrifice, a certain toughness, and it requires a strong body, mind, and spirit, and the all-important, necessary commitment to running.

Running distances isn't easy—period! That, I think, is the main reason more people don't do it.

Is Everyone an Expert?

Have you ever encountered people who talk as though they are experts on running? After decades of running, I don't consider myself even close to being an expert, although I guess I do know a little something about running since I've been doing it so long. Just having that running experience and being around the sport have given me some knowledge, perspective, and a bit of running wisdom!

But, I sometimes encounter people who aren't runners themselves and seemingly—I guess because they've read about running or know runners—portray themselves as being very knowledgeable about running. They speak as though they actually did the running or had coached the runners they talk about. Running expertise is earned over time and running distance traveled. Running expertise is the result of *doing*, not talking or reading. I think lifelong runners would agree running is a life journey which provides new experiences and ever-changing perspectives. No runner has all the answers about running, and no runner knows all there is to know about running.

Whatever the level of experience is, lifelong runners continually learn new things about running each time they run. Beware of those know-it-all runners and nonrunners!

WHY I STILL RUN

by Kent Scriber
Ithaca, New York

GETTING STARTED

I began running on a fairly regular basis more than forty years ago, shortly after graduating from college. As an undergraduate student-athlete I had participated in football and baseball, but never had much interest in being a runner.

However, that changed a few months after graduation when my brother somehow talked me into training for a local marathon (Boston Qualifier) that he was planning to run. Prior to attempting to complete this challenge, I had never run regularly, nor had I ever run more than three consecutive miles at any one time. After completing this marathon and a couple more over the next few years, I found I did not particularly enjoy the substantial amount of training that was required to participate in these long-distance events. At that point, I became much more consistent in my approach to running, and would only occasionally step up my training mileage to prepare for a half marathon or a ten-mile race, but for the most part, I began decreasing the amount of training I did. I became much more consistent with my weekly mileage, and I believe this consistency in my approach gave me a sustainable goal for running over the long term.

For many years early on, I averaged running about eighteen miles per week, and during the past couple of decades I have averaged approximately twenty-three miles per week. Over the years, these midday or early-morning jogs have become a regular part of my daily routine, and I generally look forward to them regardless of where I am, what the circumstances may be, or what the weather is.

EARLY YEARS

Obviously, my football participation ended in college and my baseball-playing days ended shortly after finishing college. At that point, I realized I needed to continue to do something athletic to remain active and maintain a reasonable level of physical fitness.

I would consider myself a competitive person, so it's quite ironic that probably the athletic activity (running) that I have performed most poorly at from a competitive standpoint has become an important and enjoyable lifelong activity for me. For several years, the challenge of improving my times over various distances did provide me with some motivation to train harder. However, even in my younger, more competitive years when I would participate in fun runs, I was at best a middle-of-the-pack finisher. Fortunately, even as a competitive person, I have seldom had the desire to go as far or fast as I could. As a result, early in my running "career" I realized, or rationalized, that it was okay for me to participate without being a top-level performer, because there were many other reasons to run.

If this hadn't been the case, I most likely would never have continued to participate to the extent that I have.

KEEPING AT IT

Over the years, I have continued to run regularly for a number of reasons. First, it is relatively inexpensive and doesn't require a lot of equipment. It is a convenient activity and can be done almost any time with or without others. When someone else participates with me, it may provide motivation to continue, as well as companionship and friendship. When running alone or with others, one can push oneself to compete/improve (or not). One of the things I have enjoyed when running alone over the years is that this time offers me a chance to reflect upon various aspects of my life, as well as thinking about and planning my day. I often use earbuds and listen to the radio, news, or music when I run. And, obviously, the health benefits, such as cardiovascular improvements and weight control (I like to eat!), are important, too. Also, I don't think there's any question it is good for one's mental health and sense of accomplishment.

Another great benefit is that if dressed appropriately, I can run in almost any type of weather. I certainly take some level of pride in the fact that I have maintained my regular runs throughout some cold and snowy Upstate New York winters.

Yes, for many years running/jogging has become a regular and routine part of my life, and I've been very fortunate not to have suffered any significant injuries or illnesses that have prevented me from participating. Over the years, many of my running partners and friends have suffered an array of orthopedic injuries that have hindered their desire to continue running or completely prevented them from remaining active joggers. I think the fact that I've never been too concerned with pushing my limits to participate (submaximal, but consistent) has helped keep me healthy enough to continue this activity for the long-term.

TRAVEL DOCUMENTATION

As I reflect upon the many places I have been able to run or jog over the years, it helps me realize how fortunate I've been to have had so many great opportunities to travel during my career. I have jogged nearly forty different states in the USA and at least a dozen different countries. These wonderful memories—that in some sense document my travel—are special, and they motivate me to continue since I always look forward to jogging in new and different places.

I have jogged in numerous regions throughout this country, including the Denali National Park in Alaska where Denali Mountain (McKinley) could be seen in the distance, and also around the Kapolei Golf Club on Hawaii's Oahu island not far from the

Diamond Head crater. In the continental United States, I have also enjoyed seeing the early-morning sun on Pikes Peak from trails in Colorado Springs, the Rockies, the Great Smoky Mountains, Blue Ridge, the Appalachians, and the Adirondack Mountains.

Some other spectacular sightseeing I've done during my jogs include New York City's Central Park, the Empire State Building, and the Statue of Liberty, many Las Vegas casinos, the STAPLES Center of Los Angeles, Anaheim's Disneyland, and the Gettysburg National Military Park. Also, I've jogged around the Superdome in New Orleans, the Rocky Statue in Philadelphia, Capitol Hill and the National Mall in Washington, DC, Baltimore's Camden Yards, and I've jogged by San Antonio's Alamo, Green Bay's Lambeau Field, and under the St. Louis Arch. I have had the opportunity to cover various portions of the Appalachian Trail (Virginia, Maryland, West Virginia, Tennessee, North Carolina) and the Daniel Boone Wilderness Trail (Kentucky, Virginia, Tennessee). This list could go on, but serves as a fun review of lots of terrific travel opportunities.

Being professionally involved with both athletics and academics throughout my career, I have also had the opportunity to visit and often jog around and explore many beautiful campuses and amazing facilities around the country. This list includes Ithaca College, Cornell University, Syracuse University, the University of Virginia, the University of Connecticut, the University of Georgia, the University of Florida, the University of North Carolina at Chapel Hill, Western Carolina University, the University of Texas at Arlington, Brown University, and the universities of Vermont, Montana, Rochester, St. Lawrence, Brigham Young, Creighton, West Alabama, and Tusculum, etc.

Around the world, my travel has allowed me to jog around the Colosseum and ruins of Rome, Venice's Rialto Bridge and St. Mark's Square, London's Buckingham Palace and Big Ben, St. Anne's/Guinness Park outside Dublin, Copenhagen's Tivoli Gardens and its Little Mermaid statue, the SkyDome of Toronto, Vancouver's Stanley Park, Beijing Sport University and its

National Sports Institute, and the Tokyo Tower with Mount Fuji in the background.

Obviously, these are lots of terrific experiences that have made my running over the years a pleasure. It's no wonder that whenever I travel, the first thing I always pack is my running gear!

GOAL SETTING AND SATISFACTION OF RUNNING

I have always enjoyed logging the miles I run/jog. As a very goal-oriented person, logging these miles always gives me a sense of accomplishment, whether it be for completing my daily, weekly, monthly, or annual results. I think this reinforces the importance of being committed, dedicated, and consistent with an exercise program that provides such wonderful experiences.

A number of years ago, I was speaking at a professional conference and sort of jokingly commented that it now takes me ten minutes to complete an eight-minute mile. Even though this has become somewhat of a self-fulfilling prophecy and I continue to go slower each year, I suspect I will continue until I'm physically not able to. Even though now completing a 10K run feels more like a ten-mile run, the feeling of accomplishment and satisfaction I attain from jogging would be difficult to replace with any other activity.

Running has been an important part of my life for more than four decades, and I would have much difficulty replacing this daily activity with anything else. These reflections should clarify why I still run.

2018 photo of Kent Scriber and the author

"Never, never, never give up."

—Winston Churchill

LOVE THE PROCESS

by Tony Cianciola

It begins with the pain, but ends with the pure endorphin release. That's what really gets you addicted to running! It doesn't happen overnight, and it doesn't happen in even a month or two months. But, when you get that first endorphin-release high after a good run, you want to continue, and from then on, it's a never-ending search for that same high.

The reason some never find that or experience it is because as runners start out, they don't want to be consistent or patient to become more proficient and efficient, and simply stop because they want results overnight. I tell people I train who want to become triathletes or better runners or better swimmers that it takes a long time to become good. And, there is *no magic bullet*. I tell them they have to be patient, as well as consistent. It *will not* happen overnight, but when that first "zen run" does come, I can almost guarantee, if they have been patient and have stuck to it, there is no turning back, and they will forever be a runner from that point forward.

For people who do not know what I am talking about when I do try to explain that, they may never understand, because it takes years of discipline, hard work, sacrifice, blood, sweat, and sometimes tears to become a *true runner*. Some start at an early age and will always be runners. Some start midlife and continue throughout their life, and finally understand what they have been missing. Some start to lose weight and turn into marathoners and Boston Marathon qualifiers. Some start because their doctor recommended it for health reasons. And, some start even as old retirees looking for something new to take up. Whatever the reason, it is always the same general response when asked why they started running: because it makes them feel good! *Plus*, they can basically eat and drink whatever they want. That's maybe the best part of the deal!

So, the author of this book, Rich Goodwin, approached me to be part of it—to be a contributor—and share some experiences I have had with running over the years, and I am happy to do so now. I decided I will also mix in some triathlon experiences, too. Let me start first by saying I feel honored to be part of Richard's book. Richard is a true inspiration to all of us runners. I do hope that in twenty-plus years, when I am his age, I will be able to run like he does now.

When my bones ache, I thank God for the feeling, because that just means He has given me the privilege to be able to run and feel alive! When I look in the mirror and see some wrinkles at my current age of forty-eight, I thank God for those, as well, because that just means I have had the opportunity to run outside and have felt the sunshine on my face for years and years. When I am *dog tired*, I am happy, because I know I have a warm, comfortable bed and pillow to lay on and feel fortunate to be able to do so.

Running has taken me to some terrific places, and I've run in all sorts of weather conditions and situations. Must places to run?

- San Francisco along the bay to the Golden Gate Bridge, over the bridge and back to Fisherman's Wharf
- San Diego along and up the bluffs at Torrey Pines Golf Course, back down along the beach and then up the Pacific Coast Highway until you cannot stand the beautiful views anymore
- The desert outside Las Vegas in the middle of summer to experience the "dry heat," or even down Las Vegas Boulevard

- A beach run in Siesta Key, Florida, Panama Beach, Florida, or any beach along the coast of Florida at sunset or sunrise (or both)
- The North Carolina Arboretum with miles and miles of trail running, hills, creeks, and mountain scenery for miles and miles once you've reached the summit

Photo of author, Lindsay Billings, and Tony Cianciola

Those are five of my favorite places to run. Also, one *must* experience a humid midday run in August in Atlanta, Georgia. Not a favorite of anyone's, I would imagine, but one you must experience nevertheless. Yes, you sometimes need to also experience those other types of difficult runs outside your comfort zone, like the sizzling summer Atlanta run when your body is drenched with sweat before you even start and the air feels so thick you could cut it with a knife.

My hottest run? Eleven miles on the track in the middle of July at a six-minute, forty-five-second pace—Ironman-type training run. There's a saying we triathletes have, and it goes like this: "You must embrace the suck." And, you have to have those runs sometimes to make you become mentally tougher. That way, when the time comes and you're hurting so bad during a run or race and pushing your body to a point where you do not think you can run another step, you refer back in your mind—in that bank of stored memories—and say to yourself, "This sucks, but it doesn't suck as bad as that run that one time on the track!" And, you can then keep going. You have put yourself through those kinds of days, where you go to the deep, dark place in your mind like in the middle of the desert—a place you don't like to go—but it is a necessary evil sometimes to remind yourself of your "mental toughness" and how you are able to endure anything.

Cold-weather run . . . another kind of "must" run is one, let's say, on a cold, rainy Sunday, mid-January, a dead-of-winter morning trail run. This is the type of day and run where you wake up in your warm, comfortable bed knowing you really don't have to get up and go outside for a run. But, you get up, get dressed, and get out anyway, because you know it's going to pay dividends come spring. Or, you wake up instead knowing you should get out to run because you signed up for an early-spring half or full marathon. Regardless, this is the type of run where you ask yourself several gut-check questions before you even get started, such as, "It's too cold and wet this morning. Why am I doing this?" Then your inner reply is, *I could just go back to bed, get some more rest, and do a treadmill run later.* Or, you might say, "I have plenty of time left before the race, and I could just skip this run and sleep in." Yes, there are a million things you could say or do to justify not going out in thirty-five-degree drizzle at eight a.m. when everyone else you know is still sleeping. Yet, despite the raw weather elements, you still go for your run!

That, my friends, is mental toughness, no matter how you look at it. And, there is just something sexy and badass about that feeling when you're out there running in the rain or even in the mud. It's knowing you're the only one who would go out for a run in those weather conditions, getting soaked, running hard, and even experiencing those burning lungs. Being mentally tough is one of the most important runner ingredients needed, because at some point you will have to dig inside yourself to meet your threshold of just how mentally tough you are. And, from that point on, you'll really be able to find out a lot about yourself. That's an important lesson running *will* teach you; it's finding out a lot about yourself that you never knew existed.

Most painful run? This is hands down the first run that comes to mind. The part I just talked about regarding mental toughness? Well, this is *that* run, where mental toughness paid off because I knew I could endure.

Let me first start by saying I could have never gotten through this run unless I had years of situations where I almost wanted to quit, but didn't—years of, as I like to say, "learning how to hurt." It takes a while, but this saying is very true. You have to learn how to hurt and learn how to "be comfortable being uncomfortable." Think about that saying for a minute. Learning how to be comfortable being uncomfortable . . . It makes sense, doesn't it? It's having an acquired feeling you learn over several years of running, or biking, or swimming, or any other endurance sport, for that matter.

So, this run and story I'm now going to share happened in Louisville, Kentucky, in late August 2007 during the marathon portion of the Ironman Louisville. The run I'm about to describe took place after a 2.2-mile swim, a 112-mile bike through the hills of Kentucky, and by the time I had started the run it was 1:30 in the afternoon on a ninety-degree August day in the midst of the Kentucky oppressive humidity. My body was already depleted, so the next twenty-six miles did not look or feel promising. When I got into the run course and crossed the bridge over the Ohio River, the streets of Downtown Louisville looked like a death march of wounded soldiers who were also struggling through the beginning of the marathon leg. It looked like it was going to be a very long and extremely difficult day for a lot of racers.

The heat had started to take its toll halfway through the 112-mile bike ride, so by the time the run started, my body was already cramping due to dehydration. All the water, salt, and potassium that I absorbed so far that day didn't seem to combat what Mother Nature had in store. It actually turned out to be the hottest day in Louisville triathlon history! Historically, this race has been an annual event taking place every August. Up until last year it had been the same weekend in August. Now, finally, after a number of years, the race organizers got smart and moved it to October—a bit cooler, to say the least.

Now, back to the story!

So, four miles into the run, it started: the worst hamstring cramps I'd ever experienced! I had to stop, stretch, and I contemplated just quitting, because with the 22.2 miles left, I thought there was no way I was going to finish this marathon. That moment was probably the closest I have ever come to quitting a race.

After taking a minute to regroup, after taking some additional electrolytes, and after some additional stretching, I started running again, still with the thought in the back of my mind to just quit. Four more miles down the road, the cramping started again. This time, it wasn't just my hamstrings, but also my quads and, believe it or not, my forearms, too! My fingers started folding in like I was being possessed, and my quads were screaming with pain.

"I'm done," I said. "I am over this crap. No more!"

At that point, my buddy who was doing the race with me came

running by. Well, I should say he was shuffling by, and I could tell he was feeling similar to the way I was feeling. We were pretty much feeling absolutely awful! There's no other way to put it. For the next sixteen miles we ran together, shuffled together, and suffered together, but not once more did I think about quitting. Now, it was no longer an option for me. Running with my friend made it easier to keep going, because I felt I wasn't alone. We were suffering together, and we would get through it together.

This race turned out to be the worst Ironman ever and the worst marathon ever! But, I learned more from this bad race than I ever have from any good race—from any "good day" of racing. And, that's what I love about running and the triathlon. Everything is a constant learning experience. You take what you get from the last race, and you use it to help motivate you and assess what went right and what went wrong, and then you can apply it to your next race.

"Have the attitude that you're going after Moby Dick in a row boat and you're bringing the tartar sauce with you." That is the slogan for my next and last segment, and the slogan I lived by in my quest for "chasing Kona." It was a lifelong goal of mine to one day be lined up treading water in the Honokohau Harbor, waiting for that cannon to go off for the 2.2-mile Hawaiian ocean swim, and to be able to compete with the best triathletes in the world at the Ironman World Championship, which is held every October in Kona, Hawaii. In order to do that, though, I would need to qualify in another Ironman distance race.

Ironman Kentucky didn't seem to pan out that hot August day. Remember when I said it takes a long time to get good and it takes patience, sacrifice, and consistent training? Well, all of that is *true*. Six Ironmans later, I found myself in that harbor treading water, listening to the beat of the Hawaiian drums on shore, looking below, seeing the divers with cameras filming all the antsy legs and feet treading water, and waiting for the cannon.

But first, let's back up eight years. First, there was the Ironman Wisconsin. My goal was to finish and learn, with no expectations about time. Second was the Ironman Kentucky. There, I had some expectations, but still entered the event with a bit of naïvety; I was relatively inexperienced. My third Ironman event was the Ironman Arizona. I had every intention of qualifying for Kona. I was prepared, fit, and the temperature was perfect on that November day. But, I did not pace well on the bike and the wind changed directions, so on the last lap I pushed it too hard to stay on my projected time, and it came back and bit me sixteen miles into the marathon, because it caused me to have to slow down and blow up a bit. That, in turn, dropped my placing out of the qualifying spot. It was a good race altogether, just a bit "short," so I said, "Next time, dammit!"

Fourth Ironman was Kentucky again. This was the race I entered with the highest expectations, but ended up having the worst race ever (the race I described earlier). At this point, Kona became a mission! The fifth attempt took me to the Ironman Florida. I intended this to be my last try, because chasing the Kona dream was starting to wear on me both mentally and physically. I had put everything I could into this event's training. I mean, *everything*! I left no stone unturned, had spent thousands of dollars on nutrition, chiropractic care, hyperbaric-chamber recovery, an amazing coach, a committed training partner—the one who bleeds with you and is willing to sacrifice with you, and who has been there with you in the trenches. I had sacrificed a lot and had put every ounce of effort into this race preparation. If it didn't happen this time, I was going to have to put my dream on hold for a few years. All business this time.

It turned out to be a perfect-weather day. I was in the best shape of my life and felt more prepared than ever. It was the perfect day in all respects, and I was convinced and confident everything would come together. It seemed magical!

As it turned out, I had my second-best marathon ever, including open marathons. I was coming off a 112-bike ride to finish the day. It turned out great, with me finishing twelfth overall out of 2,400 competitors and second in my age group out of 450. I had secured one of nine qualifying spots in my age group for Kona next October! I had finally done it! I had accomplished my goal by qualifying for Kona, and a big part of my dream had become reality.

But, I still needed to cross that finish line on Ali Drive in Downtown Kona by the harbor next October 2012. That's the infamous finish line where they put leis on you as you cross the finish line in what's considered the world's hardest endurance event. I still needed to recover from the Florida race, regroup and assess my training plan for next year, get through the holidays, meet with my coach and set training schedules and activities, and most importantly, stay healthy for next year and hope for no setbacks. Patience was now going to be the key for going into next year's training.

Now, fast forward to March of 2012 and beginning training for Kona . . . so I thought. But, it was about that time my worst nightmare came to reality. After a weekend of moving tree stumps from a storm cleanup, I woke up that following Monday morning and fell straight to the floor. I had herniated a disc.

You can imagine my first thought when I went to the doctor and he looked at the MRI and told me the news. His initial statement to me was "You're race season is pretty much over." He then said, "With months of rehab ahead and possible surgery, if rehab doesn't work, I do not see any way that you would be able to start training again this year and be able to put your body through the rigor that your training entails."

And so, the rehab began. Fortunately for me, I had an amazing and knowledgeable physical-therapy staff that helped to take care of me and my injury, and they made a point to make sure I would be at the start line in Kona. June came, and with consistent therapy I found I was able to gradually start training again and by July 1 was almost full tilt into the heart of my Ironman training and Kona preparation.

I got to the start line in October, crossed that special Kona finish line, and had accomplished my ultimate goal. From a choppy washing machine of a 2.2-mile swim in the Pacific, to a scorching and windy 112-mile bike ride through the lava fields along the fifty-six-mile stretch of the Queen K. Highway and back, and a 26.2-mile run on asphalt hot enough to melt the soles of your shoes, to the finish line ten and a half hours later, I can say without a doubt that all the sacrifice, all the pain, all the sweat, all the money spent, and many hours training was worth it.

The Kona experience and accomplishment was the single most worthwhile life goal I had ever achieved. Maybe someday I'll go back and line up on that starting line again in the Honokohau Harbor. Until then, I'll keep trying, and I'll embrace the journey that comes my way.

My parting words are "NEVER, NEVER, NEVER QUIT!"

Photo of Tony Cianciola crossing IRONMAN finish line (Photo courtesy of Tony Cianciola)

CROSSING PATHS

"Before becoming an endurance runner, you first need to experience what it is to endure."
— Richard C. Goodwin

I think another wonderful facet of lifelong running and being part of the greater running community is the opportunity to revisit familiar places and see or hear from others who have directly, indirectly, or even unknowingly been part of your running life. I think one way to visualize this is to imagine a series of concentric circles, with the subject runner being at the center, and then various running events, training places, running buddies, acquaintances, and other running-related connections being shown on surrounding rings. Those appearing on the closest circles/rings represent people, places, and events experienced most frequently, while less frequent experiences and interactions appear on successive, outer circles/rings.

As a lifelong runner, I've occasionally experienced the unexpected, and here's an example. Generally considered to be the "father of modern running" and catalyst for the first running boom, the legendary and great American runner Frank Shorter will forever be remembered for his astonishing 1972 gold-medal, marathon-winning performance at the Munich Olympic Games. Coincidentally, I happened to be serving on active duty in the US Army in Germany at the exact time he was making running history. Days prior to his historic marathon run, he was seeking safety and protection at the Olympic Village in response to the brutal terrorist attacks. Simultaneously, just up the road from

Munich and in direct response to those attacks, a couple of soldiers were ordered to signal immediate heightened readiness and response. I happened to be one of those soldiers.

Then, in 1993, Frank Shorter was in Upstate New York to run a sponsored 10K race. After the race, he came to my restaurant and mingled with fellow runners for some time before leaving and heading out. But, before leaving, he agreed to have his picture taken with my five-year-old son, so I snapped a picture of them standing together outside the restaurant front door.

Now retired, I've taken some time to look back and revisit some of my past running events and experiences, sift through old photos, and try to put some order to it all. I came across the picture of Frank Shorter and my son, and enjoyed seeing it again and re-membering the day we were together. Seeing that picture brought back a very special and wonderful memory.

I had purchased a copy of Frank's recent book *My Marathon: Reflections on a Gold Medal Life*, read it, loved it, and gained con-siderable and meaningful insight about Frank Shorter, his life, and his running life. After reading his book, I felt a sense of addi-tional connection to him and was inspired to try to reach out to him, express my profound appreciation for all he's meant to so many of us in the running community, and ask him to please con-sider signing that special photo of him and my son.

Back in 1972, I wasn't a runner, just a soldier. But starting around 1977, I began to run, and have run fairly consistently ever since. So, when I reached out to Frank Shorter in 2017, I felt a life-long runner kinship with him and was comfortable trying to get in touch with him. Frank did receive my letter and picture of Richard Jr., and he graciously signed the picture and sent it back, along with a handwritten note! Amazing!

Back in 1972, while an army soldier, all I knew about Frank Shorter was that he was a famous runner, an Olympic athlete, and Olympic champion. Back then, I never, ever thought I would ever meet him or that I would become a runner. In 1993, after his 10K run, he became a very special guest and most welcome visitor to my restaurant. I had become a marathon runner by then, having completed my first in 1981. And, the time we spent together and the picture I took of him with my son served to connect us through running.

In 2017, after he and I reconnected and corresponded, he has once again become part of my world of running and is included among other terrific friends I have in the running community. I've lived in and visited many different places, and I've run on different tracks, trails, sidewalks, and roads up and down the East Coast, but in my wildest dreams, I never thought I'd ever cross paths, connect, and correspond with the great Frank Shorter.

"It is never too late to be what you might have been."
—**George Eliot**

Photo of Frank Shorter and Rich Jr., 1993

"The power of imagination makes us infinite."
—**John Muir**

LOOKING FORWARD

Years ago, a very good friend once told me, "Don't look back. Look forward and move on." I think it was said in the context of right or wrong, good or bad, for better or worse; we make life decisions and end up living by the choices we make. The question he raised was, "Do we really gain much from second-guessing ourselves and the decisions we've made?"

Is it fair and even sensible to say "If only I'd done this," or "I wish I'd done that instead"? Most of us have been there and experienced that, and my friend Tom understood that when he shared those simple words of wisdom with me. He told me twenty-twenty hindsight and Monday-morning quarterbacking are easy. He said we all make mistakes, we learn from them, we adjust and adapt, and should just move forward.

Since then, and after becoming a consistent runner, I've found running forward and looking forward go hand-in-hand. Running helps me be optimistic. It helps me look beyond the day's activities, see the future, solve problems more effectively, and rarely do I now find myself dwelling in the past or stuck in the mud alongside my past mistakes. Moving forward down the road or around the track keeps me focused and looking forward. Running helps me to be positive and ready to tackle new challenges, and to find ways to navigate through life's many situations, challenges, and related problems as they come my way.

If you run consistently over time, I think you'll have a smile on your face as you look forward, too!

YOU CAN GO HOME

There's nothing quite like visiting family and friends in and around the town where you grew up. Seeing those old, familiar places and reconnecting to your childhood past brings back many memories, some good and maybe some not so good. But nevertheless, it's the place you were first raised, and it's the place where you first attended school and maybe even first played sports.

One easy and convenient way to see those places is by car, but there's nothing like a run down the same sidewalks you walked as a kid, and even walking provides an intimate view of things. But, I prefer running through town up and down sidewalks, roads, into and out of parks, on and around athletic fields, and passing by my old home, as well as jogging past old friends' homes.

Maybe you can't move back, but an occasional visit can go a long way to soothe the soul! Yes, you can go home, and should . . . and running the town is a great way to see it again and reconnect.

Photo of my "hometown track," a great place to run when visiting family and friends

Runners Are Everywhere!

Now that I'm retired, I'm out and about more and have extra chances to visit with people in places other than those from my current hometown and former workplace. It seems wherever I go, runners abound! I notice doctors, lawyers, teachers, students, business owners, people from a variety of occupations are runners and distance runners, and it's been great meeting and connecting with them, listening to their stories, and hearing about their passion for running.

Yes, the running community thrives in all shapes and sizes, at all ages and performance levels across the USA and around the world!

THE RUNNING CYCLE

I view my running activity as a cycle of sorts consisting of runs of different lengths and difficulty spread out over two-year periods of time. Why two years? Well, it's because I allow for an ebb and flow along the way, and I build in time for rest and occasional relaxation and recovery to offset periods of greater intensity, increased mileage, and effort.

Most marathoners I talk to about their running plans tell me they build mileage systematically and incrementally over time, culminating in their marathon run. I like to start with a 5K race, followed by a 10K, a half marathon, and lastly with a full marathon scheduled toward year-end somewhere between October and December. Then, beginning the next year, I plan a half marathon to run around March, followed by a summer and early September 10K, a 5K, and then following the 5K, I start adding mileage again, gradually building my mileage base so I prepare to run a full marathon in December. I find it's so much easier and welcoming to finish a year-end marathon run with a mileage taper by training for a half marathon and progressing toward races of lesser distance—the 10K and 5K.

The mileage base I've built the first year works for me and helps me wind down a bit, recover, yet do well in the shorter races the second year of my running cycle. Then, gearing up again at the beginning of the new two-year cycle is easier to do, and I feel relatively refreshed doing it and actually look forward to running higher mileage again. You might want to give it a try and see how it works for you.

> *"Cross training/weight training is a smart way to extend running life by helping to slow down or even stop the loss of muscle mass and strength due to aging."*
> —**Richard C. Goodwin**

> *"A champion is someone who gets up when he can't."*
> —**Jack Dempsey**

WANT TO WIN AND HATE TO LOSE?

I've always been interested in what it is that separates average runners from those runners who exceed their own performance expectations. Completing the race is important, yes, but finishing the race above performance expectations or finishing among leaders is running with distinction, and some runners have figured out how to do it time and time again.

Am I suggesting all runners should run with that kind of intensity and drive? Of course not! There are and will always be different levels of runners and performance, and that's the nature of the sport. But even with that being said, I think some runners—some athletes, some businessmen and women, people from virtually all professions and walks of life who succeed at a high level—don't want to fail, and at the same time are equally determined to succeed with distinction. I think it's that combination of working extremely hard not to fall short while simultaneously working just as hard or even harder to accomplish or exceed goals and objectives that provide the special fuel and fire needed. Maybe it's purposeful running with a conscience. Maybe it's that "never quit or give in" quality and capacity that propel runners forward to and through the finish line, enabling them to meet their time goals even though they're hurting, tired, or not feeling their best come race day. Maybe it's part of our runner journey and the process of discovering who we are and what we're made of.

Over time, and as we evolve as runners, we learn about ourselves, the event and distance, and what we can really accomplish when we muster all our resources—when we do the best we can with the will to see it through to the finish line.

> *"Rewards from running begin at the end of your comfort zone."*
>
> **—Richard C. Goodwin**

Ever Have a "Bad" Day?

Are you and other runners *running machines*? As runners, do we sometimes think or believe we can run hours at a time, day after day, and never break down? Do we often experience running as being effortless and an extension of our natural being, rather than some sort of tedious and monotonous activity? Good days of running and racing can fill us with a sense of invincibility, and we're fed with the notion "the more we run the better!" That is, until we experience what has often been referred to in running as having a "bad" day.

What's a "bad" day of running? Well, it's more or less when the machine—the human machine—either breaks down, overheats, needs a tune-up and new parts, or just plain has to have some shut-down time, rest, and recovery. It can also happen, for instance, on race day, when the temperatures are way off the norm or when there's torrential rain, sleet, ice, snow, wind, or all of the above. It's also when the runner fuel tank feels empty. And, it can be because of many other factors. Feel free to add them and list them here!

As runners, we all have probably had "bad" days of running along the way. We have discovered we are not machines, and that if we run ourselves too much (whatever that subjective threshold is), then in time we will experience the inevitable injury and breakdown. I have seen it at every level and intensity of running and for all ranges of age groups.

At our local high school, it's becoming more and more common to see cross-country and track runners wearing boots around the school because they've had stress fractures. Why did they sustain stress-fracture injuries? They tell me they ran too much; they overdid it. Consequently, they sometimes find themselves lost for all or part of the season. I can assure you when they experienced that injury, they truly had a "bad" day of running.

I think knowing when to push and back off training comes with running experience. It comes with learning to pay attention to your runner body—knowing fatigue and responding to it appropriately, getting the right amount of rest, nutrition, recovery time, and sleep, and seeking medical advice and assistance, physical therapy, etc., when needed. All this contributes to healthier, happier, and sustained, consistent running without breakdown and injury. That, in turn, results in many more "good" days of running!

RUN ALONE, WITH ANOTHER, OR AS PART OF A GROUP?

Most of the runners I know tell me they prefer running by themselves. But, many also enjoy running with others, so for them it's largely situational. They prefer running on their own because they have a customized, personalized, and purposeful workout schedule. Some say they like to run by themselves simply because they want to spend some uninterrupted time with themselves and get in touch with their inner-selves without having the distraction of others and having to engage in partner-runner conversation or group-runner banter.

However, running with a partner can be a great sharing experience. I've run with others and have cherished that time together, because it often provides me with additional life insight, problem-solving opportunities, and creative thinking. Plus, sharing the road with a running partner has helped me get down the road and back with seemingly less effort. Running with someone can be rhythmic. Running with someone who has a similar gait, cadence, and runner rhythm is being in sync. It's when running partners are moving together harmoniously and not a word is spoken between them . . . that's when you can hear, see, and feel the running partnership, and it seems to reinforce each runner's movement, efficiency, and really seems to lessen the effort.

I think group running could be characterized as herd running.

It's as though runners become part of a herd of runners. Anything goes here, but if you're among runners with similar speed and pace, you can feel right at home with them. Group running fosters team spirit, and being part of a team can also be an exhilarating experience, especially when each member shares a common and purposeful goal. Competition may seep in, but that's okay, because members test one another and performances can improve as a result. The same can hold true in partner running. Partners can find occasion to push each other, staying together—just rallying the other to pick it up, move forward, upward, and onward together!

Photo of the author and Geoff Martin, New York Road Runners Central Park ten-mile winter race

"Train for a marathon with someone else and make a lifelong friend."

—Richard C. Goodwin

Run with Someone and Never Run Alone

Over the years, I've had the good fortune of having running partners and having trained with them for one event or the other—sometimes marathon training over periods of years. If you've run with others over an extended period of time, you know there's a connection that's made, and often it becomes a long-lasting relationship.

Running partners not only share their runs, but they also often share their thoughts, feelings, problems, insights, and other life aspects. Because of various life events, those running relationships probably won't last a lifetime . . . or will they?

I've found when I'm out running early a.m. by myself, I sometimes think of my former running partners running beside me. When I summon the memories, they're with me in spirit, and it seems they always will be. Though it's just me running, I've discovered I really never run alone, because it's the memories of my running partners and all the wonderful runs we shared out on the sidewalks, trails, and roads that remain every new step of the way.

Photo of the author and friends Geoff Martin and Jose Roman

The Mechanics of Running

We often read or hear about distance-running technique: what we should and shouldn't do, what works and what doesn't, and I think you'll agree there may be as many different approaches to running and ways to run as there are runners! I mean, one size or "way" to run doesn't fit all runners, because of the different ways we're made, the different ways we prefer to move, and so on. Yes, generally it's agreed there are some things all runners absolutely should and shouldn't do, such as runners shouldn't pound their feet into the ground when they run, and runners shouldn't eat gigantic pizzas right before running marathons, and runners should actually train for the races they run . . . obvious things like that!

So, when referring to the mechanics of running, I mean how our bodies move when we run, regardless of differences in running style and look. Remember erector sets? I sometimes think our body posture resembles the general composition or structure provided in erector sets. We sometimes move in robotic ways—in stiff and choppy ways. When we enable our joints, cartilage, our ligaments, tendons, and muscles to work in unison with our skeletal support, we add that much needed synergy, flexibility, fluidity, and we soften the mechanical look and result, making the running stride and movement more efficient, effective, even effortless as our upper and lower bodies work together, facilitating a glide forward, one stride after the next. The upper body and lower body move differently, yet their joined contributions to running are necessary and codependent.

I like to think of the upper body as the tabletop, with the lower body—from hips on down—providing the legs, support, and stability to the upper body (tabletop). I've discovered running is easier and more enjoyable when I consciously visualize the combination of the two both working together to move the entire body forward, not so much in an up-and-down motion, but forward in a combined glide with feet staying under head, shoulders, and hips just above the ground, pushing off and moving forward. I visualize the muscles, tendons, ligaments connecting with, softening, and directing the body forward in a relaxed manner. Relaxation is the key, because it allows fluidity in the repetitive motion while unleashing running power. Believe me when I say allowing your muscles, tendons, and ligaments to do their parts results in less pounding and effort in motion, less grinding forward with robot-like, choppy movement, and instead provides relative ease and running strength through whole-body effort.

Imagine yourself systematically "unhinging" your feet and ankles from a more rigid or even locked position as they move forward from one foot strike into another, and as they push off, gliding forward to the next upcoming distance. You may discover you'll cover more distance per stride with less effort and discomfort along the way. I now appreciate the mechanics of "natural" running and have learned running probably shouldn't feel or look overly mechanical, and I suppose that just might be the best mechanics of all!

ICE!

Please don't underestimate the power of icing sore muscles, particularly sore calves, feet, and ankles. When your feet hurt after runs, there's nothing like placing those tired and sore feet on top of, around, underneath, or in a bag of ice for several minutes to find much needed relief to help quell that soreness and swelling.

Don't hesitate to use ice or wait too long to use it for those inevitable aches and pains. Shortly after showering, grab a bag of ice, get a comfortable seat, apply the ice, and then sit back and enjoy. Do it a couple of times a day, if you can. You'll find the healing and good feeling will be there for you . . . and those aching feet of yours!

> *"For first-time marathoners, it's more about getting to the finish line. For experienced marathoners, it's about arriving on time to a scheduled appointment with the finish line."*
> —Richard C. Goodwin

THE DAY AFTER THE MARATHON

So, you've trained hard, made it to the start line, and run through to the finish. You've successfully completed your first marathon (**YEAH!**), eaten your postrace dinner, and are now fast asleep. All is well and good!

... That is, until you wake the next morning and discover some surprise aches, pains, and maybe worse as you try to move from the bed to the bath (and beyond). Yes, you may have conquered the marathon distance the day before, but now you find yourself feeling pain and discomfort in new and unexpected places.

The aches and pains can often be quite severe a day or two after completing the marathon, so expect the unexpected and do your best to respond to your body's ills in the days ahead. Most of the time, the aches and pains aren't serious and they'll pass, but sometimes you'll develop a serious postmarathon physical issue or injury that will require a doctor's attention. You know your body, and you will have a good feel for the extent of the injury, and you will usually know whether a doctor visit is the route to take.

Be patient with yourself, especially after completing your first marathon, and give the body a few days to heal and feel more itself again. On the bright side, by the time you become a veteran marathoner, you'll know more what to expect and how to react to most postrace aches and pains.

Pre- and Post-Marathon Routines

Most marathoners have their own pre- and post-race routines—the collective preparation, logistics, strategy, and all that's involved. Here's some things this veteran marathoner has learned to do:

- I arrive to the event at least one day prior; two days prior, if at all possible
- I pick up the race bib the day before, not the morning of the race
- I check out the start and finish areas
- I review the course map, topography and elevation changes, water and aid stations, etc.
- I lay out the race clothes, shoes, and socks the night before and attach the race bib using safety pins. I have a pretty good idea about the race-day weather so I'll know what to bring with me and what I think I'll want to wear. I also write my emergency information on the reverse side of my race bib.
- I eat a fairly light dinner the night before the race and drink water, but don't overdo the food-and-water quantities

- I set the alarm (yes, I bring my own alarm clock) to wake up at least two hours before the start. I arrange for a hotel wake-up call, too.
- When the alarm goes off, I get up, and after the first bathroom visit, I have breakfast and coffee. I have my prerace breakfast meal and drink well before getting dressed. I check the weather and temperature outside, what it currently looks like, and what's expected later on during the run. I drink water, gather the supplements I'll carry with me during the race, and make sure I carry them so they will be readily accessible during the run. I use my hotel/home bathroom as best I can prerace to help avoid using the less comfortable portable toilets before or during the race.
- I'm sure to apply petroleum jelly to toes, other foot parts, and other body areas where I expect rubbing/chafing/friction during the run
- I make sure I have family/friend supports in place the day of the marathon. I take a room key/card, phone (the running stretch belt and pouch helps here).
- Depending on the weather and temperature, I try to get to the start area to line up somewhere between fifteen minutes to a half hour early. I gently stretch in my room prior to going to the start area and stretch again at or near the start area when I arrive. I warm-up as needed, but am careful *not* to run a marathon warming-up before actually running the marathon! In short, I don't overdo the warm-up.
- Once there and ready to go, I start the race with a positive outlook, clear mind, and spirit of determination
- I usually stop at the water stations and drink

- I eat my supplements every forty-five minutes or so to add carbs and energy as I move through the race
- I pace myself and remember it's a marathon, not a 10K, and also remember it's probably going to get pretty tough from eighteen miles through to the finish
- I'm sure to cross the on-ground timing strips I encounter along the race course so my official race progress will be recorded and counted
- After finishing, I'm sure to get my finisher medal and much deserved refreshments. I've earned them! And, I add some protein to my postrace dinner to refuel those strained and tired muscles.
- I shower, rest, and recover, hydrate, eat, and tend to my newfound body aches and pains
- On returning home, if driving, I take my time and allow for some stops and stretch breaks, as needed
- I check my results and record them in my running log, notebook, or scrapbook. Pictures were most likely taken during the race, so when they become available, I usually buy one or two as keepsakes!

"Want to qualify for the Boston Marathon? You will, in time, if you don't slow down as much as the qualifying times do."

—Richard C. Goodwin

Plantar Fasciitis

Several years ago, I went through the pain, suffering, and healing process associated with having plantar fasciitis. During decades of running, I'd never had plantar fasciitis before, so this was a big surprise.

It hit me suddenly toward the completion of the 2016 Kiawah Island Marathon. The pain was sudden, sharp, and strong, but somehow I just pushed through to the finish line. I ended up hobbling around right after finishing and pretty much for the next several weeks.

Eventually, I went to see a podiatrist who diagnosed the plantar fasciitis, and he told me what to do. I followed his recommendations, and after ten weeks my left foot and heel finally felt close to normal again.

This is what he encouraged me to do. First, he told me to stay off my foot as much as possible and elevate it periodically. He told me to ice the area, and suggested I try rolling a frozen bottle of water back and forth under the foot. That way, he said, I would benefit from both the cold and the massage provided by the bottle. Then, he told me to stretch the immediate area and even the connected calf area very slowly and gradually by moving my weight forward while keeping my foot flat on the floor. He recommended I do the stretching exercise at least twenty times throughout the day. We discussed running shoes and future prevention of the plantar fasciitis, and he recommended I run in shoes with a heel-to-toe drop of approximately twelve millimeters or greater.

I found this injury to be pretty serious, and I am hoping it won't recur. I think with proper stretching, along with periodic icing and massage, I should help prevent future problems.

If you get plantar fasciitis and need some help, I recommend you consider seeing a doctor who runs and/or treats runners, and who is familiar with it. The podiatrist I saw is a runner, and was very familiar with the nature and full extent of plantar fasciitis. I believe it made a big difference!

RUNNING KEEPS US GROUNDED

In this age where many of us don't seem to know where fact ends and fiction begins, where increasingly people are spending more and more time on social media, and where people are being pulled in so many different directions they sometimes end up losing touch with who and what they are, running and the world of running can often provide solid antidotes. The connections provided through running are solid, both on individual and community levels. Runners establish and maintain a self-connection and extended connection to the community and world around them, because they see and hear what's "inside" and "outside" when running. There is nothing artificial, inflated, unreal, made up, or untrue about traveling minutes, hours, and miles down the road or around the track. It is as sound and solid as the ground under foot. Running is *real*, and it reminds us who we truly are.

A Special Fall Run

by Lindsay Billings

Every fall in high school, around October, my cross-country team was fortunate enough to have the opportunity to travel to an out-of-state race. We would spend the night in a hotel, four to a room, and get to race new teams instead of the same rivals we'd always fight it out against back home. Then, we would stop at an amusement park later in the afternoon. It was a highlight of the season—the only reason some of the JV kids were even on the team—and the source of many fond memories for me.

My senior year was going especially good; we had upgraded from a meet in Florida to a more competitive meet in South Carolina, and for the first time in weeks all five of our top scorers were healthy and in shape. We were a team on the rise, and we knew the weekend could earn us national attention . . . if only we could beat the Riverside girls.

Riverside was a South Carolina team famed for year after year of success. Whenever they graduated their best runners, they always seemed to have equally successful underclassmen to fill their places. But, my girls and I had been training hard and knew that while winning would be a challenge, the feat was possible.

On top of the team goals, my own ambitions swelled. This race is run on the same course that, later in the year, hosts the national qualifier. The previous year I'd had a shot at making it to the national meet, but caught up in the excitement, I disregarded my race plan and ended up struggling in the last mile, and eventually I got passed at the finish line to miss qualifying by less than half a second. This would not only be my chance to redeem myself on that course, but running it in the lower-pressure environment would help me figure out how to run it smarter so that I would be ready in November for that year's national qualifier.

The high stakes and excitement of the trip were all my teammates and I talked about in the week leading up to the departure. Our ambitious goals were about to become reality—that is, until Mother Nature stepped in.

It started raining about Wednesday that week, and the rain only got heavier from there on. All over the East Coast, rain turned into storms, which turned into a full-blown hurricane, and Charlotte was hit badly. We were supposed to leave on Friday, but Thursday afternoon our coach came to the practice to deliver some bad news. The race was cancelled.

We were heartbroken, knowing we'd have no other chance to prove ourselves until after the regular season ended. I knew this would hurt my chances of a better race in November. I went home from practice pouting and cranky, and stayed that way through the rest of the evening.

I woke up Saturday, and my first thought was, *I should be racing now.* But I wasn't, and so instead I had to get my long run in. It was still bucketing outside, even at my home in Georgia, and I looked upon the raindrops, dreading an hour and a half of being beneath them. Generally, long runs are my favorite runs of the week, but that day it would just be an uncomfortable reminder of the cancelled meet and my lost goals.

Right before I headed out the door, my phone rang with an invitation to meet my teammates at the lake, where they had decided to run together. My first instinct was to turn it down, because generally, my pace was faster than theirs, and my disappointment about the weekend was no excuse to slack off. Also, I knew the trails at the lake would most probably be entirely flooded, whereas the streets by my house all had storm drains.

Plus, those trails were a thirty-minute drive away. In the end, though, I just couldn't bear to face the rain by myself, so I drove to the lake, intending to run again on my own later if I had to.

Photo of Lindsay Billings, ACC academic honor roll and cross-country runner at Duke University (Photo courtesy of Lindsay Billings and Duke University)

The trails were flooded. Not just flooded, they were raging rivers, muddy pits, and waterfalls! The rain kept pounding down on us as we started. Mud flew everywhere, kicked up with every stride, and we had to slow down just to stay on our feet and navigate some of the trickier spots. Before long, I realized there was no way "fast" was happening, and wisely devoted my full consciousness to staying on my feet. As it turned out, even that wasn't a realistic expectation, as each of us tumbled and slipped over the muddy surface. But, in the end, it all turned out to be the most fun I'd had in ages!

All five of us girls were laughing the entire time at how ridiculous the rest of us looked being all muddied up and struggling over the terrain. We were a mess! Within minutes we were soaked to the bone and covered in mud, and felt like children playing in a summer storm. The cancelled race hung in the back of my mind, but I found myself almost thankful I wasn't there, because I ended up going to the lake and loved being in the middle of the woods, soggy and gross, and connecting with my best friends.

The pressure and promise of competition is thrilling, but can be all-consuming at times. There is so much more to running than winning, or proving yourself, or going as hard and as fast as you can. Running is not just a competitive sport; it's also a pastime and social event, a chance to be outside, and an opportunity to get up and get moving in the company of people you care about.

Runs like the one I had with my friends on that very rainy day are few and far between, usually unexpected, serve as a reminder of why I started running in the first place, and provide extra motivation to never give up.

Photo of Duke University cross-country runner Lindsay Billings enjoying a relaxing weekend run (Photo courtesy of Lindsay Billings and Duke University)

What Running Means to Me

by Cara Reilly

When asked what running means to me, the image, word, and person that comes to mind is my dad. He has instilled in me a passion for running, and most importantly, he's been the best running partner a daughter could ever ask for.

He started his running journey in high school. But, it wasn't until he was offered the opportunity to go back to school and have his college education supported through running that he learned how incredibly talented he was and how much he enjoyed running. While attending college and earning his college degree, he was a business owner, husband, father of two little girls, and also the top runner on his college team—all culminating for him at the age of twenty-eight. When I think of my life now, I try to imagine how he accomplished all he did. I'm amazed! Looking at it now, I know it was due first and foremost to his strong faith, and then his incredible work ethic, support system, and true and genuine love of running.

Our training together started when I was quite young. I use that term "training" loosely, as I could not—and most of the time still cannot—come close to keeping up with him. Instead of running, I would ride my bike alongside him as he ran. Just as we do today, we would talk about everything under the sun, from school, to sports (the majority of our conversations), to just life in general. Even in the silent moments, when we were too tired to talk, we just enjoyed each other's company.

As I am writing this, we are in the midst of training for our fifth marathon together this spring, and looking to complete our sixth one in the fall. Unfortunately, because we now live in different states with over one thousand miles distance between us, we are unable to physically train together, but he continues to motivate, support, and push me, and I hope I am doing the same for him.

What he has given me, the many life lessons I have learned, the rare opportunities to run side by side through Boston, New York City, St. Louis, and every other place we have visited are and continue to be the highlights of my life. He has taught me a unique perspective and way of looking at life. Running has granted me a perspective that I may have missed otherwise had I not decided to take that first step with my dad. For me, it is the truest form of demonstrating what can be achieved through the combination of hard work, mental strength, and patience.

Photo of Cara Reilly and her dad, Art (Photo courtesy of Cara Reilly)

Running has shown me what the body is truly capable of, and it has taught me how to push to and over that edge (what an amazing feeling—when you are finished, of course!). Running has opened my eyes to what an amazing gift from God our bodies are, and to never take my health for granted. I am truly fortunate to be able to run and, more importantly, to share my running experiences with someone else.

Being the ultracompetitive person I am, PRs and finishing races at or near the top of my division are things I am constantly striving for. However, what matters most and what I remember most clearly are the amazing times my dad and I have shared through running. The bond we've created, the memories we've made, and the excitement of what's yet to come are what I cherish and value most, and I could never thank him enough for that.

That's what running means to me.

MARATHON,
MY SINCERE FRIEND
by Sunjune Lee

I have been running for ten years since I started two-to-three-mile baby jogging a month before Thanksgiving 2008. Meanwhile, I have now run twenty full marathons and twelve half marathons, several 5Ks and 10Ks, and am expecting to run my twenty-first full marathon someday soon. Ironically, the more I run, the more I am scared and nervous in anticipation, because I know what the pain will be like. I do, however, humbly take it as part of the fun in running.

I was born and grew up in South Korea, and most of my education was about pursuing high academics to be equipped to survive in such a competitive and closely knit society. I was never exposed to anything I could do physically just for fun. Surprisingly enough, when I could spot many runners easily here and there in my new neighborhood when I moved to America in 2001, I instantly loved seeing them, but couldn't imagine I might become one of them.

One day, I wondered what made those many people dare to run early in dawn or late in dusk, cold or steamy hot, or rain or shine. I was so curious, but in the beginning, I had no courage to come forward and ask for information. Once I knocked on the door of running, however, it wasn't a big deal. All I needed to do was just put on my old sneakers, shorts, and tank top, and that was it. It was as simple as that, even though I added pricy gear like a fancy watch and a pair of nice sports sunglasses later for style and support.

No sooner than I began running, I was surprised to realize that I was enjoying every moment very much, even while suffering almost being out of breath. Living in another country is never easy, and I am self-conscious and tense 24/7. My Asian face and Korean accent always single me out no matter where I go or what I do, but in running I am naturally distracted from who I am, and instantly get lost in stepping one foot forward and another next. To my embarrassment, I feel sometimes even superior to others who don't run. It gives me a small, secret confidence and pleasure which I haven't experienced since my twenties. This tiny conspiracy encourages me to get out of my comfort zone and keep running.

Another thing I like about running is that it pays me back exactly how much effort and time I put in. No free luck or random disaster are applied. It is fair to me. This strictness keeps me on rigorous discipline and regular practice. I strongly rely on this stubbornness and perseverance; it keeps me back on the track even in the middle of disappointment, depression, or stress.

Marathon itself is like a sincere, old friend who will never betray or leave me, if only I don't desert it. What a relief to know that I will never be alone, because I know for sure I will never stop running, and Marathon will be there for me all the time.

Photo of Sunjune Lee (Photo courtesy of Sunjune Lee)

WHY I RUN

by Beth Whitehurst

I run because I love being outside, putting myself in nature, being able to travel through beautiful countryside, and cover more distance than I could by walking. Most of all, though, running *without* headphones allows me to enjoy my own present mind and company.

It helps me to be my own best friend.

Photo of Beth Whitehurst, white cap (Photo courtesy of Beth Whitehurst)

A Time to Reflect

Every so often—and for some it can be a rare occurrence—runners get injured, and they're sidelined for an extended period of time as a result of the injury. Those of you who have experienced this unfortunate and even painful interruption in running routine know how difficult it is to go from runner to nonrunner status. Hopefully, the injury is temporary, and over time it is remedied and heals 100 percent. It's happened to me, and I've found cutting back on running is difficult enough, but not running at all is really tough to do. I just tell myself to be patient, seek treatment and medical advice, and allow the injured area to heal, period, no questions asked!

It becomes a necessary mind-over-matter situation of restraint and self-control. I use this time away from running to reflect on prior years running and glance longer term to future training and racing. It's tough slowing down and stopping, but I try to turn that negative into a positive by gaining perspective about my running.

I guess it's like taking an "injury vacation" away from running—although the vacation could be an extended one, much like taking an extended vacation from work. I think this time away can, ironically, be beneficial for runners, because an injury-related "vacation away from running" provides additional time for perspective about self and life usually not found through everyday activities.

It can be a time for reading, too. It can be an opportunity to pick up and read books and magazines about running and runners. There's lots out there filled with motivational and interesting information about runners and running.

Yes, being sidelined from running can turn out to be a valuable time for reflection and renewal of spirit.

Reach out
to Other Runners

One of the joys of running is you automatically become part of a greater community of fellow runners. That runner community often includes friends, coworkers, club members, relatives, and others.

Make time to reach out to some of these people, offer encouragement and support, share stories about your running, and talk about what's working and what isn't. You will be glad you did!

Running the Canal Route

by Geoff Martin

Early in my running days—1979—with a few 5K and 10K races in my logbook, I set my sights on the New York City Marathon. Nothing could interfere with my training that spring and summer: training the length of Riverside Drive, on the rolling hills of Central Park, all in the service of making it through those 26.2 miles of my newly adopted home city. My wife and even my two young children knew my priorities.

At that time, I was on a fellowship at NYU when a friend and I chanced to browse one of the public bulletins in our academic building. There at the bottom was a neatly typed notice:

APARTMENT EXCHANGE
DO YOU HAVE A NEW YORK APARTMENT
YOU WOULD LIKE TO EXCHANGE
FOR AN APARTMENT IN
VENICE
FOR THE MONTH OF AUGUST?
PLEASE TELEPHONE: *(Italian number listed)*

"What a lovely idea," I commented to my friend. "Wish I could go."

He listened. I described the troubles of traveling with a five- and three-year-old, let alone the costs of the flights. And, of course, I would have a hard time getting in my hill training for the marathon in a city that was—almost by definition—one of the world's flattest. August was planned to be my peak month for the October 21 big run through the city.

"This is perfect for you," he retorted. "You have the time off from work, a nice apartment on the West Side, and you may never have this chance again—with no hotel bills!" No runner, he. There was no falling back on my training excuse in this discussion.

I dialed the long-distance call to Venice, and a cheery woman speaking near-perfect English answered. Yes, her apartment was still available, and she would come to New York with her young daughter. A short chat convinced her that we would be reliable tenants. My wife was easily persuaded to make the trip.

Venice in the summer is made for children: boats running up and down the canals, no cars (or traffic), lots of souvenir shops, and pizza around every corner. We settled into our routine of morning sightseeing, afternoon naps, and dinner at outdoor cafés. Our son Colin, on his own, started sketching in churches and art galleries. Our daughter Liza loved running the city, up and down steps, cheerfully trying to keep up with her brother.

This fully built city has a modest park at St. Elena on the eastern end, so I resolved to run there, flat and tiny though it was. Early in the morning, running through Piazza San Marco free of tourists was refreshing. The park wasn't bad, either. There was a circuit route of about a quarter mile being used by other morning runners.

After a few laps, Giorgio, a Venetian man of my age, asked if I was a visitor. We communicated in French and my halting Italian, mostly. His Venetian Italian was strange to me, even if I had been a good Italian speaker! Giorgio explained to me that a group of his running buddies met early every Sunday morning to do a tour, usually 12K, and sometimes with an option for an additional 8K. Invitation accepted.

The next day—my first Sunday—I was welcomed by four guys happy to be joined by a New York runner. We ran through the winding streets, making unannounced turns through tiny *passaggios* into quiet neighborhoods rarely ventured by tourists. This was a regular intrusion, apparently. Elderly residents taking in Sunday morning along the route waved, calling out the names of one or another of the runners. I brought up the rear, wondering when the next tiny street would abruptly appear. Every minute or two, one of Venice's arched *ponti* bridges would pop up in front of us to allow our transit over a canal. Twelve steps up, twelve steps down. A minute later, a bigger canal, a bigger bridge: twenty up, twenty down.

I fell further behind.

"*Stanco*, Martin?"

Yes, I was tired. They laughed. An easy bridge—six up, six down—and a sharp left into a dark alley. More greetings. Not exactly waiting for me to catch up, they just urged me on. My first 12K in Venice was long enough. (I later learned that there were forty-seven *ponti* in the first run.)

The next Sunday, a slightly different route with more stone-arch bridges and their shallow, sloping steps. I still struggled, but agreed that the 8K add-on would be okay this time. This day I could talk with them in limited Italian. The men were mostly laborers. Otello worked the overnight shift on Murano, the glass-making island. It was his job to keep the furnaces stoked so they would be ready for glass-melting in the morning. All of them knew a Venice I could never have dreamed of seeing.

By the third Sunday, I was breathing more easily, keeping up with the group, conversing a little better, and learning the route, deftly negotiating the bridges, and even waving to some of the now-familiar spectators. By now, our family had been in Venice nearly three weeks, and we knew our way around the tourist spots pretty well. We felt like locals. My buddies kept asking me about the *maratona*. Was I ready? They were glad to hear that Venice was helping.

One weekday morning, after my customary solo run around the small park, I stopped at a spiffy bakery shop near San Marco to pick up some croissants to take back for breakfast. It was a humid morning, and I must have looked it; almost *nobody* walks in central Venice in a soggy T-shirt, let alone into this bakery.

A young woman waited on me with obvious disdain.

"Quattro croissants, per favore."

Just then, a huge tray of freshly baked goods appeared from the kitchen on the strong arm of Carlo, one of my running buddies. "Martin!"

"Carlo!"

My four croissants were handed over, along with a big smile from the clerk as she listened to Carlo explain who this sweaty tourist was. I waved *ciao* to Carlo. *"Domenico prossimo!"* (Next Sunday!)

The last Sunday, I was ready to run. I led the group (seven of us) over bridges and down alleys, along canals, and around churches, and they kept up. They were doing me no favors; my Venetian running was up to snuff. That final week, with extra solo runs and with Giorgio, I had logged forty-seven miles. When we finished, the group wished me well with my running and asked if I could send them marathon T-shirts from New York. Otello gave me some small glass horses, a bird, and a snail from his shop. Giorgio added a glass fish. They bought me some coffee, and we said farewell.

When I returned to New York, I found some suitable T-shirts in various sizes and mailed them off. On October 21, 1979, I clicked off my first marathon in 3:39.

I had no trouble with the hills.

PUMA-FALMOUTH ROAD RACE
13th Annual
August 18, 1985

Photo of Geoff Martin and the author, 1985

It's a Family Affair

Let's face it: running can and sometimes does impact those closest to us—spouses, significant others, and children. Yes, it's great when families run together, and it's terrific when families are supportive of their runners. Sometimes, though, that's not the case. The runner-family dynamic can resemble the old, stereotypical "golf widow" relationship: husbands out on the golf course several times a week spending hours and hours practicing and playing golf while their wives and children find themselves home alone.

Over the many years I've run, I have learned to try and schedule my runs around quality family time so my training and race time don't conflict with family time and family activities. It's not always possible to avoid running-family scheduling conflicts, but I've tried my best to plan my runs accordingly. When it comes to the "big event"—the race selection and the race itself—I usually select the races, race sites, and venues I think will also be interesting for my wife. Race-related overnight stays in nice hotels and condos where the race locations happen to be in beautiful, scenic, and interesting places also helps. Staying with friends provides a very nice alternative by allowing time to reconnect in a comfortable and supportive setting.

Everyone's different, and there are as many different runner-family situations as there are runners. But, as we're chugging ahead on our daily runs and in our races, let's try our best to remember the "family factor" and try not to leave them behind.

"Run races alongside your family and friends. Watch them run, and you will see them for who they truly are."
—**Richard C. Goodwin**

ARE RUNNERS REAL?

I think we live in a time when the lines of fact, fiction, reality, and fantasy can be fuzzier or more blurred than ever before. Largely because of capabilities provided by and through the use of social media, some people create an alternate reality about and for themselves. For some—and certainly *not* all—select pictures are displayed, written comments and stories posted and shared, activities and travels cited, and so on—all attempts to portray themselves, their lives, families, pets, and friends favorably, seemingly even perfect in some cases. Some people have purposely utilized social-media platforms to create and display an almost idyllic, alternate life that's materially different from their true-life reality.

I think some of these people are exaggerators and attention seekers, and I also think they seek heightened levels of recognition, self-importance, and relevance not normally experienced or provided, earned, or deserved in their "real and true" daily lives. But, that's just one runner's opinion, and I guess I should probably stop now and leave the "real and true" analysis of all this to those who really study, know, and follow social-media dynamics: the psychologists and psychiatrists of the world who understand the uses, effects, distortions, and abuses of social media.

But, before moving on, I'll add one more comment. I've been told some of the more extreme social-media users (or "junkies") spend hours each day meticulously crafting their realities and figuring out how to carefully and best display themselves and their life activities in the most favorable light for select others to see. It seems those people are far more interested in time spent creating their personal, artificial realities than they are expanding and applying their "true and honest" selves. What, then, is real and what is not real? I will leave that answer to you.

However, experience has shown me that running is real and running isn't an illusion. It isn't an illusion to run a 10K race in under fifty minutes. It isn't an illusion to complete a half marathon in under two hours, and it isn't fantasy or fiction to grind through the entire full-marathon distance in under four hours. Those are true and real—*earned*—and the times of completion and recognitions received are well deserved.

All my "real" friends have decided not to participate in social media, period. They are well-grounded; they are comfortable in their own "real and true" skins—strengths, weaknesses, flaws, and shortcomings included.

Do runners ever participate in social media? Of course, they do!

My guess, though, is most runners do tend to portray themselves accurately and as they and their life activities truly are. They probably tend to "show it" and "tell it like it really is!" At least, I like to think so.

My closest friends happen to be accomplished athletes, and most of them are runners. They have (or have had) successful athletic careers. All are action-oriented. They are doers! They complete their runs and other athletic activities just like they complete their daily-life tasks. They are reliable and consistent about how they accomplish both. The miles they run are earned, not given, and they don't expect handouts. They are grateful, and they prefer to earn their money, property, and life experiences. The runners I know are self-reliant, industrious, intelligent, dependable, authentic, determined, energetic, capable, empathetic, honest, generous people who have developed a robust overall stamina and enthusiasm for life.

Yes, I have found runners are real! Their deeds and actions stand alone and speak for themselves without the assistance of social media.

KNOW WHERE THE DOGS ARE

It goes without saying, runners need to be aware of their surroundings so they can be safe on their daily runs. Safety is most important, whether runners find themselves running in cities or suburbs, in parks or on trails, or even when they run in their own familiar neighborhoods. And, it's also important to find out where the vicious dogs are roaming!

Yes, even dogs on leashes can be dangerous to runners, especially when the leashes are those retractable, expandable types. Some dogs are very sneaky, and appear to be harmless and even friendly until you start to run past. These are dogs that are smart, wily, and skilled at providing runners with a false sense of calm and safety. They are good actors, and they know it. They will mark and measure runners and hold them in their sights, and at just the right time, they will lunge to try to take a chunk out of runners or knock runners down. Even when the dog misses, it's startling and could result in the runner making a sudden, unanticipated reactive movement in the wrong direction, causing a slip, fall, and injury.

Narrow sidewalks can be the worst if this situation presents itself because of the limited available space for escape. So, common sense dictates runners should take a wide berth around dogs whenever possible, or learn to avoid them all together.

Recently, I heard about a runner who happened to be out bike-riding through a park area when a large and vicious dog came out of nowhere and knocked her off her bike and onto the ground. The dog bit her, and she ended up needing medical attention and follow-up procedures, including having stitches and rabies shots, and it ultimately took her months to recover.

Don't get me wrong. I love dogs! I do believe they can be our best friends, and let's try to keep it that way when we take our daily runs!

WHAT'S THE TIME?

Many years ago, at about the time I began training to run my first marathon, I became quite interested in classical music and started to listen to it and learn much more about it. I love classical music, period, and fondly remember my first real exposure to it at age five when I heard a radio broadcast of the New World Symphony in kindergarten class. It was amazing, powerful, and I got a good case of goosebumps listening to that performance by the Rochester Symphony Orchestra. Thank you, Antonín Dvořák and Mrs. O'Donnell!

Years later, I purchased concert tickets to hear the Boston Symphony Orchestra play at its Tanglewood summer home near Lenox, Massachusetts. The great Eugene Ormandy was scheduled to be the guest conductor for that July evening's performance of Beethoven music. At the time of that concert, Maestro Ormandy was nearing his life's end. He appeared frail, but he somehow marshalled all the vigor the music and musicians required.

At one point during the outdoor concert, thunder and lightning erupted. It seemed as though Maestro Ormandy had summoned synchronized clamor at exactly the right time, and he had captured it and placed it precisely into the symphony and music score itself. It was incredibly eerie. During those moments, the entire audience was spellbound; you could literally hear a pin drop, because like me, I think others in the audience realized they were experiencing a once-in-a-lifetime phenomenon. We *knew* Maestro

Ormandy was conducting the music and musicians, but now it seemed he was also conducting the weather and the sky above! I'll never forget it.

Sometime later, I read about Maestro Ormandy's uncanny sense of time and timing. Apparently, he possessed an innate ability and "internal clock" that provided him with a mechanism to accurately track and record time.

I think runners can also develop their own internal clocks and sense of time as it relates to running, pace, and distance covered. Years of running provide experience and a keen sense of time travel, a predictor of how long it takes to run from point A to point B. When that happens, you can leave the watch at home, because your internal clock will keep time for you.

APRICOTS?

Sometimes, it seems as though distance running and leg cramps can go hand in hand. Runners who have experienced leg cramps in the midst of a marathon run know it's something they wish had never happened, and it's something they'd like to quickly forget!

Prevention is the name of the game when it comes to cramping, and distance runners do what they can to prevent leg cramps from occurring. Hydration, electrolyte levels, potassium consumption, carbs, sugars, foods, and nutritional ingredients are all reviewed, monitored, and factored into the marathon-training period, marathon-day preparation, and the marathon run itself!

About ten years ago, I had experienced some cramping during a couple of marathons but thought I had planned and prepared adequately for cramp prevention. It was disappointing, difficult, painful, and I was confused and didn't have an answer. Shortly after, I was shopping at a local grocery store and thought I'd run it by (no pun intended) the head pharmacist, who I knew happened to be a triathlete and distance runner. Fortunately, he was working that day, and he had a few minutes to see me. When I told him my plight, he replied, "Apricots."

I said, "Apricots?"

Then he said with absolute certainty, "Yes, apricots." He said from his experience, eating dried apricots had served as an effective measure to help prevent leg cramps because of apricots having a relatively high concentration of potassium and other beneficial nutrients. Apparently, eating dried apricots had worked for him!

So, I thought I'd give it a try. Well, I ate a handful of dried apricots periodically throughout my next marathon training and the week before the race, and I made sure I ate several on race-day morning. Sure enough, no leg cramps, and since then I've been sure to periodically eat apricots and haven't had leg cramps since. Adequate and proper training, hydration, and nutrition are all important factors, of course. But, all things being equal, I think it was eating those apricots that made the difference for me.

Apricots aren't for everyone, I know. Some runners have told me "Yuck!" when I've mentioned apricots to them. But, other distance runners who have eaten them have reported apricots had indeed worked for them, too!

A word of caution here: If you do try apricots, please don't overdo it! A small handful should do the trick. And, be sure to drink something—preferably some water—after eating apricots to help wash them down and also to help moisten the mouth.

If you do try apricots as an anticramping remedy, I hope they'll work for you, too!

THE "WELL-ROUNDED" RUNNER

Don't you appreciate writers of movies, plays, and novels who not only provide interesting and entertaining stories, plot development, surprise, and momentum, but also provide for and reveal character change, growth, texturing, and rounding as the story progresses? At the beginning, both the story and characters are often portrayed in relatively simplistic ways, and the story itself may move rather slowly and deliberately. It's as though the story and characters are just warming up, just getting started. But then, over time and plot progression, both the story and characters change, revealing more and more, and by story-end receive a well-earned "Wow!" from the reading or viewing audience. The characters—the protagonist(s) and supporting cast—become more relatable; they gain and provide a greater sense of dimension, color, texture, and purpose as they evolve.

Runners also change over time. At the start, most runners are just putting their feet to the ground, getting their feel for running and deciding whether or not they like it, and sometimes wondering whether or not they're even cut out for running. Over time, consistency enters in, adjustments are made, and many runners start to think running is for them, and it's an activity they enjoy and want to continue to do.

Then comes the first race, more races, and races of increasing or different distances, and so on. Runners move through their first year of running and beyond, and if all goes well, they ultimately evolve into long-term runners or even lifelong runners! Not every runner does, but some runners do stick with it over the long haul and eventually learn to accept running as being a vital component in their lives. They experience ups and downs along the way with some good and some not-so-good days, but through it all, they gain invaluable runner and life experiences and perspective.

They change over time. They become "well-rounded" runners.

"The Chairman of the Boards"

The year 1981 was when I ran my first marathons: the Long Island Marathon and the first of my three New York City Marathons. It was a very good year, partly because it was the year I "officially" became a marathoner and long-distance runner. The "running boom" was clearly upon us then. Running had become enormously popular because of the prominent contributions and inspiration of so many people, including Frank Shorter, Bill Rodgers, Grete Waitz, Fred Lebow, Jim Fixx (author of *The Complete Book of Running*), and others. People were hitting the roads, sidewalks, tracks, and trails all across the USA in quest of going the distance and improving fitness.

The year 1983 was another good year of running for me. I ran my fastest NYC Marathon, and it was also the year I purchased two tickets to go see the Millrose Games. I lived sixty miles north of New York City at the time, but was very familiar with the Big Apple because my work frequently took me there. I invited my friend and marathon-training buddy to go with me, and he agreed. After all, how could he turn down a free ticket to see the Millrose Games? And, he lived in the city, not too far from Madison Square Garden and the Millrose event venue. What could be better? Runners watching runners! Sure, it was midwinter, very cold, and the games were scheduled for the evening, but we figured we'd just bundle up, brave the elements, and go.

As we made our way down the snowy and slippery sidewalk and into Madison Square Garden, we had no idea what we were about to experience. We walked in and found our seats. They were high above the indoor track's near-corner location, where milers would make their final turn and race to the finish line. This mile run wasn't just any indoor mile. This was the historic Wanamaker Mile. Some of the finest indoor milers would compete for the prestigious Wanamaker Trophy.

Various track-and-field events preceded the Wanamaker Mile event. Sprinting, relays, jumps, and pole vaulting all took place, and they were super fun to see. And, as time went by, I could feel anticipation and excitement brewing throughout the arena, because the time for the running of the Wanamaker Mile was near.

Then came the announcement of the mile-race contestants, and the name of one runner stood out from the rest and was given thunderous applause from the spectators in the jam-packed arena. It was the announcement of Irishman Eamonn Coghlan!

Now, just before the race was to begin, the anticipation was palpable, and the arena atmosphere was electric as the runners took their places. "Runners, take your place! Get set . . ." and then came the *crack!* of the starting pistol.

Off they went.

Around and around they went, and with each passing lap on the banked, wooden track, I could hear the spectator unrest, chatter, and noise building and building. That was because with each and every lap, spectators could follow the time elapsed and start guessing the finish time. What they couldn't know with absolute certainty was the winner and the winning time.

The race continued, and Eamonn Coghlan held his position near the lead. The leader at the start was what is commonly referred to as the pacesetter, or "rabbit." It is the pacesetter's role to set a brisk pace and to help the rest of the field of runners settle in before dropping back and out of the race. The "rabbit" did his job moving the pack of runners forward.

Suddenly, Coghlan pushed to the front by ramping up his

speed. At that very moment, the spectators erupted! They had been watching his every move and instantly responded to his surge to the front. Coghlan started to pull away. He had timed his move perfectly, and it was clear he wanted the lead!

He was now in control of the race. It was his race to win. I asked myself in amazement, "Can he hold his sizzling pace, and if he can, what on earth will be his finishing time?"

He continued to crank forward with amazing determination, further exhibiting his incredible speed and endurance. I could hear the pounding of runners' feet on those wooden boards, and then came the signal for the bell lap. The roar increased as Coghlan made his final turn and headed toward the finish line. It was astounding to see him pull further and further away from the field toward the finish line. The spectator cheering was deafening and widespread throughout the entire arena!

He won, and crossed the finish line to the sound of a thunderous applause in a time of 3:54!

I'd never witnessed anything approaching that level of spectator excitement. The best runners were running, and this was truly running at its best. The applause continued during his victory lap as he waved and connected with the adoring crowd.

Yes, I will always remember attending the Millrose Games and seeing those talented track-and-field competitors. And, I will best remember being introduced on that cold, wintry night to the spectacular, legendary Eamonn Christopher Coghlan, who has earned the right to be forever known as "the Chairman of the Boards."

IS IT IN THE SHIRT?

Often times, runners prefer to run in a favorite shirt on race day. I happen to be one of those runners. My favorite shirt is a light-green, Frank Shorter–brand singlet, and I wear it in most of my races unless it's a very, very cold and windy race day with temperatures around or below freezing.

For me, it's just not any shirt. It's a Frank Shorter–brand and styled shirt, and in my mind, it gives me extra speed, endurance, and determination when I'm racing in it. I actually think it helps me get through tough patches during marathon runs and I run with more overall confidence. I believe I can better handle whatever comes my way during those grueling 26.2 miles when I'm wearing it.

How many races have I worn it in? Many, and I've got the safety-pin holes and shirt marks to prove it! Pinning those many race bibs to my Frank Shorter singlet has made those many, many holes, and for me, that just adds to the shirt's provenance.

I guess one could say the shirt, like the runner who has worn it these many years, now shows signs of wear and is a bit scarred, battered, and bruised. Am I planning on replacing the shirt anytime soon? Not a chance! Maybe I will never replace it. Why would I? For me, there's still something magical about it—how it fits just right, and how it's been there for me and with me on those many race days. It's always come through for me, and it continues to help inspire me to do my very best each and every time I race.

And, maybe that's because the shirt has a little bit of Frank Shorter woven into it.

Photo of Green Race Singlet

WHAT WOULD YOU DO?

In 1983, I had trained to run the New York City Marathon with one of my former running buddies. He and I usually ran together several times weekly over our lunch breaks. We saved our long runs for the weekends, and we did those on our own. Being a couple of thirty-four-year-old amateur runners, we were pretty fast back then, routinely running somewhere between a 6:30 and 7:30–per mile pace. We factored hills and intervals into some of our runs, so some days we moved faster, and other days we slowed it down a bit. But, we pushed each other, challenged each other, and helped each other with our marathon preparation.

Sometimes, we and our families got together for a dinner or two, and our wives and the kids enjoyed that special social interaction. But, make no mistake about it, Jose and I were all business when it came to doing our serious running. We were passionate about our running, worked very hard. We were dedicated, determined, and goal-oriented, and each of our runs was purposeful and in keeping with our marathon-training plans. We prided ourselves in our fierce running consistency.

Over that yearlong training period, we got to know each other very well and supported each other both in our running lives and also in our personal lives outside of running. We knew each other's strengths, weaknesses, ups and downs, and lifted each other's spirits and provided extra motivation as needed.

As we got closer to race day, we reviewed our current situations, progress, and race strategies, and we both felt confident about our chances to do well and meet our time goals and race objectives. We also agreed we should not try to run the race together. We recognized running side by side would be difficult, if not impossible to do, because we knew there would always be an element of uncertainty—unpredictability—that came with running the 26.2-mile marathon distance.

Race day finally came! We met at the holding area near the start and walked over to our start positions. That much we could and would do together! The race start was upon us, and the canon fired and off we went.

We moved very slowly at first, and it remained slow going over the first several miles into the race. Back then, it was all "gun time," because the "chip time" wasn't used. And, because of the vast number of runners, it took extra time for us to move into a relatively comfortable runner position and settle into our space and planned pace.

Jose went ahead and I soon lost sight of him. I was moving along fine with relative ease, and I was cruising forward in my "zone" until I approached a point somewhere between sixteen and seventeen miles into the marathon. It was then I unexpectedly saw Jose broken down on the right side of the road. He was on the ground hunched over, not moving, and when I got nearer to him, I could see he was hurting and distressed. My concentration was abruptly broken and my focus turned suddenly to my friend and training partner, Jose. I asked myself, *Should I stop, or should I run on? What should I do?*

Well, for me, there really wasn't any doubt. I stopped when I got to him, put my arm around him, and then tried to assess his situation. He was quite despondent; he seemed broken and beaten, and he told me he couldn't go on. He told me he didn't want to run anymore. He was incoherent.

While I consoled him, it had become abundantly clear the time was ticking by and the race clock was moving on, and on, and on. I knew I was falling behind on *my* time goal. However, at that moment, what mattered most to me was trying to help Jose as best I could. So, I talked more to him, encouraged him, and was encouraged and surprised to see he started to come around and out of his beaten, distressed state of emotion and frazzled frame of mind. I told him, "Jose, you can do this! You can keep going!"

At first he refused, but after some more encouragement, he said he would give it a try. I lifted him up, held him upright, and instructed him to try to walk with me. He did, and we walked together, slowly at first, and then a bit faster as his legs stabilized under him. I got him to eat a couple of orange slices and drink some water. Then, amazingly, he said he would like to try to run again! I said, "Great," and saw him start to shuffle forward at a very slow and deliberate pace. After traveling some distance together and after I could see he was jogging again, I told him I was going to run ahead, and I would see him at the finish line. So, I ran ahead and felt pretty good about stopping to help Jose regain his senses, recover, and get back into the race.

Photo of Jose Roman, the author, and friends, 1983, post-New York City Marathon

Looking back on that experience, I've asked myself if I would do the same thing again if faced with a similar situation. And, although I'm thirty-six years older now, and in some ways more experienced and a bit wiser, I've concluded I would. Even though running is, by its very nature, a relatively solitary endeavor, and even though marathon-finisher times and goals are super important, I couldn't and wouldn't—in good conscience—then or now pass a friend on the road who is in distress without stopping to try and help out.

Jose did eventually complete the race, although he ended up in one of the medical tents afterward. So, I ask, if you found yourself in a similar situation, what would you do?

LOCAL RACES

Understandably, many runners set their sights on running some of the various and major "big city" marathon races staged across the country and around the world. The same holds true for the half-marathon and 10K distance races. Most are exciting, big-time events with so much swirling around them: sights, sounds, and activities to tap into. Running them and being part of that entire experience can literally turn out to be life-changing.

But, along with the many positives of being part of the big-race experience are some potential negatives, such as the planning and organization needed and the time and expense involved. Yes, unless runners live in or around the big cities and those big-city races, it can be very expensive to travel to, stay in, and eat there. It may be a major event full of excitement, but accompanying the major prestige is often that major price tag of getting there, staying there, and then returning home after the race. For some runners, it can prove to be overwhelming and unaffordable.

Local races can be terrific experiences. What they may lack in participant and spectator numbers is more than made up for in their hometown feel and flavor. They offer runners convenience and a relatively inexpensive way to be part of organized and sanctioned races. They may be smaller in scope, but they provide a much bigger intimacy factor. Runners usually have lots more room to spread out on the course and move around throughout the race, and it's usually a much calmer and quieter experience altogether. The familiar faces of local volunteers tend the water tables, along with the prerace and postrace areas, and help provide the food, drink, and the necessary runner support and race information.

Runners see their friends and colleagues from their community and often feel more relaxed being among them. Additionally, many of the local races are tied to worthwhile causes and local charities, and runners who enter can end up making a meaningful contribution. They can walk away feeling extra good about the event and their run.

So, consider the small, local races, too. Sprinkle some into your race planning and calendar. You will be happy you did!

Photo of the author, 2016 Publix Georgia Half Marathon

ARE YOU A CLYDESDALE?

If you are a runner who has always chased behind much slimmer, lighter, and faster runners, you have experienced what I have, and you've faced the grim reality you will probably never, ever be able to run that fast, no matter how much training and dieting you do! But, have hope, because as I've discovered, there is a category for heavier, more "muscled" runners called the Clydesdale division!

I completed the Harwich (Massachusetts–Cape Cod) Cranberry Harvest Festival 10K race, entered and competed in the Clydesdale senior division (190 pounds and up), and took second place in my age grouping of fifty and older! What is great about this race and concept is heavier runners are recognized, respected, and given their place and a fair shot to compete against others like them. Clearly, race organizers recognize the need and appropriateness to give heavier runners a fighting chance, a fair chance to have a competitive race with weight factored in.

So, if you are a heavier runner who trains hard, eats right, but still tips the scales at 190 pounds or more, please know there may be competitive races and a Clydesdale division out there just for you, like the annual late-September/early-October race held in Harwich, Cape Cod.

I can say from personal observation that in all the races I've run over the past forty years, few runners my weight or heavier have passed me by or finished in front of me. Thank goodness for the chance to compete in the Clydesdale division in the Harwich run, and I thank race organizers for factoring weight classes into their competitive divisions.

Maybe this concept will catch on and be added in other races around the USA and around the world. I hope so for all my fellow Clydesdales out there in the running world.

Drinking on the Run

Water stations are critical. Agreed?

Whether runners opt to drink the plain old H_2O or a fancier sports drink containing carbs, sugars, and electrolytes, it's especially important to hydrate along the way when running half-marathon and full-marathon distances. To a more limited extent, the same holds true for 10K races, particularly those run in warm, hot, and humid weather.

I've seen various hydration methods and contraptions used in distance races, including fancy runner "belts" containing various bottles and liquids. Most runners I've observed over the years drink up at the hydration stations and tables, which are typically staged in one- or two-mile increments throughout the race. Runners grab little cups of water and/or sports drinks, and they try drinking on the run as they pass through the stations, all the while attempting not to spill. Or, they drink during an actual brief stop to help assure no spilling!

The runners carrying bottles of liquids in their runner belts trudge right on through the hydration stations, because they've got a full and ready source of hydration available to them whenever a drink is needed. Sometimes I see a few beltless runners who hand-carry bottles with some sort of liquid inside. So, whatever the hydration strategy, there's a hydration method to choose from.

I prefer carrying a special concoction of flat cola, some sports drink, and water (equal portions), and I drink as I run from a handheld, small-sized, plastic bottle. I make sure the mixture is refrigerated and cool (or cold) when the race begins. Then, as I run, I drink as needed, and usually find it lasts the first thirteen to fifteen miles of a marathon or the entire half-marathon distance.

When I've emptied the bottle during a marathon race, I make sure to drink water the rest of the way at the designated hydration stations. Sometimes, I will even stop briefly and add water to my empty bottle and then drink from it best I can for the remainder of the marathon run. It usually works for me.

Now, I understand the taste I've created in my mixture isn't for everyone, but I've grown accustomed to it. I can tolerate it, and I know I'm getting the water, electrolytes, carbs, and sugars I need. Is it a bit inconvenient to carry the bottle and liquid contents? Yes, it is. Plain and simple, it can seem like a nuisance at times! But, when I weigh the pros and cons, I figure it's helping me overall and worth that minor inconvenience.

The bottle size I like to use is around eight to ten fluid ounces. And, the bottle shape I use is narrow enough so I can grasp it and carry it easily in one hand. As I run, I pass the bottle back and forth between hands to relieve whatever strain I experience in either hand. In a full-marathon run, I usually discard the bottle during the last four or five miles of the race and drink any additional water at the remaining water stations. I sometimes find that carrying the bottle along the way helps relax me, because it's relatively light and it reduces the tension I sometimes feel in my hands and fingers.

If you've been experiencing dehydration during your long runs, or you've been experiencing leg cramps, you might consider trying out my mixture and method. Maybe it will work for you, too!

THE DREADED KNEE INJURY

Now, I'm not a doctor, and this isn't intended to be medical advice or a diagnosis from me to you. But, believe me when I say if you ever sustain a knee injury from running—and by that I mean more than a minor twinge, slight passing pain, or discomfort—I think you should take it seriously and probably seek medical attention, and the sooner, the better!

Why? Because it will most likely worsen if you continue to run.

Trust me, I've been through it and can attest it doesn't matter how tough you are or what your pain threshold is. Eventually, you'll see either the front of your knee, back of your knee, and/or sides of your knee swell—most likely from fluid buildup—and then your knee will stiffen to a point where it will feel "locked," and all that will most likely be accompanied by increased pain. And, the longer you continue running on your injured knee, the longer it will take to heal.

Fortunately, I ended up seeing an orthopedic doctor who happened to also be a runner—someone who understood running, runners, and knee injuries. She provided an accurate assessment, diagnosis, treatment, and follow-up advice.

Be prepared to rest, elevate your leg/knee area, and apply ice frequently. Physical therapy may follow. You will probably be sidelined for a period of time, but hopefully you won't need surgery. If you can, find out what caused the knee injury in the first place. In my case, I found out it was a combination of muscle weakness, imbalance, and pelvic and skeletal misalignment. Either or both could be contributing factors, or it could also simply be a result of the repetitive pounding associated with running.

Early intervention, receiving prompt and proper treatment and follow-up therapy, and then being patient with yourself to help allow healing and recovery to take place are key here, and will hopefully facilitate your return to running the roads again sooner than expected!

STARTING OVER

Running again after having been sidelined because of a running injury isn't always easy and shouldn't be rushed. If the injury has resulted in being sidelined from running for an extended period of time—say, eight weeks or more—then it often becomes increasingly difficult and challenging to get back into prior running form. And, even when the body has recovered from the running injury, it now has to relearn movement, toughness, and stamina. Until it does, too much, too soon can result in a postrecovery injury either to the previously injured area or even to new areas.

Taking time and gradually starting back into running again slowly and consistently will probably work best. It may take a couple of days of new running to offset each day of previous fitness level lost, so thinking longer term and being patient about running postinjury and recovery should pay dividends and should be planned and accordingly woven into future training, race goals, and objectives.

In some ways, running after being sidelined for an extended period of time can seem like starting all over again.

"Today is the only day. Yesterday is gone."
—**John Wooden**

KIDNEY STONES!

Some believe learning to run longer without drinking water, even on hot, humid, sunny days, is a way to toughen up and teach your body to run farther without needing water. Maybe that works for some runners, but from my experience, that kind of water deprivation is an extreme position and training technique that can result in serious dehydration, loss of energy, and worse—the dreaded formation of kidney stones!

Anyone who has had kidney stones knows it's very, very painful, and it can be debilitating when kidney stones form and then decide to move around. Even relatively small-sized kidney stones (or jagged-shaped gravel moving around and out of the kidney) can cause serious discomfort, aggravation, and even excruciating pain!

I know that to be true from personal experience. Instead of not drinking water when running, I've been told by doctors to drink water often and as needed in order to stay hydrated during runs, and especially when running through those hot, humid summer months. I've tried the "don't drink and you'll learn to run without needing water as often and you'll toughen up" method, and it did result in a series of kidney and kidney-stone problems. Now, I'm careful to hydrate before, during, and after runs. And, I also drink lots of water with lemon throughout the day not only to help prevent the formation of kidney stones, but also to help assure I'm adequately hydrated and flushing toxins out.

On the other hand, I recognize runners should be careful not to drink too much water, because that can lead to overhydration problems. But, I can't emphasize this enough: unless runners are into pain or know they will never run the risk of having kidney stones, it's probably better they work at staying adequately hydrated, especially during those dog days of late summer!

Believe me when I say you don't want kidney stones, and you don't want to experience the pain they cause when they move around!

RUNNING WITH DEER

Recently, at around 6:30 in the early morning while on my usual school-parking-lot loop run, three deer came up unexpectedly, then jumped *over* the school's chain-link fence, landed, and then moved down into the student parking-lot area and walked slowly over toward the high school gym. I continued jogging, moved right, turned the corner, and saw the deer were on my immediate left—one road removed—and they just moved along with me as I neared the gym entrance. They stopped, then I stopped, and we stared at each other. Their ears spread wide as they faced me.

After admiring them for several moments, I decided to resume my run, and the deer continued their jaunt across and down through the student-parking area toward the athletic fields. Now, I ask, "How's that for an unexpected, early-morning welcome surprise?"

Just one more amazing, wonderful example and reminder of why I run!

"Run as if success is inevitable."
—**Richard C. Goodwin**

PRS DON'T COME EVERY DAY

Part of the thrill of running is running faster! And, over time, runners have plenty of chances to set personal goals and set new, faster times. Achieving those faster times and setting personal records, or "PRs," is the result of dedication, hard work and sacrifice, proper training, getting faster, and running faster on race day. The more we run fast, the faster we get, and shaving minutes or seconds off runs over time rewards runners with those much coveted PRs.

But, it's inevitable for runners to peak at some point, and over years and years of running, older runners know—this runner included—those fastest times usually become a thing of the past. It doesn't mean we can't still run relatively fast and hold our own and sustain our performance when compared to others our age. PRs take on a new and different meaning. We adjust our thinking and expectations, and compare our performances to others in similar age and division categories. We measure ourselves against our own prior performances and also compare what we do to others in our same group of competitors.

With consistent effort, we can set new PRs in our new age categories. It's possible and realistic with extra effort, smart training, and outstanding overall preparation. No, PRs don't come daily over extended periods of time, but they can and do still come in a new context as we age as runners. The incentive to improve is still there for runners who put in the work. And, above all, it takes patience.

Yes, new PRs may not come frequently for older lifelong runners, but improved times are there for the taking in the context of age and division groupings.

Moochers and Freeloaders

Did you ever meet people who repeatedly ask for help from others and make little effort to help themselves, or people who habitually take advantage of others' generosity, or people who borrow money and "things" without intending to repay or return? These are people who have made sponging off of others their own form of art. They have an uncanny ability to identify and latch onto givers, and they have an insatiable appetite to get all they can, and they continue living their lives with a seemingly limitless entitlement mentality. They are the "takers" of the world, and it seems the more "givers" give to them, the more the "takers" become empowered to take more, and more, and more. They are the moochers. They are the freeloaders of life.

However, I have yet to meet a consistent lifelong distance runner who is a lifelong moocher and freeloader. The distance runners I know take pride in earning things, not taking handouts. Their marathon and half-marathon runs (and runs of other lengths and durations) are fully earned, not handed to them. A strong work ethic, sense of sacrifice, commitment to running, and self-reliance are woven into and extend throughout their personal and professional lives.

Consequently, what lifelong runners gain through running isn't taken for granted, but received with a keen sense of gratitude and appreciation with humility. Yes, running isn't about mooching and freeloading. No, I don't think you'll see many lifelong distance runners lined up at the start lines for mooching and freeloading life events.

Running, Investing, and Instant Gratification

The longer I run, both in terms of distance and days, months, and years, the clearer I see both the connection and disconnection between running, investing, and life expectations. Pace of life has increased, changes occur more often, the internet continues to provide information at super speed, attention spans continue to shorten (partly because of technology's constant intrusion and influence, and peoples' increased tendencies to multi-task). Impatient investors look for quicker money returns, and over the past forty years, I've increasingly noticed the characteristics of having patience, understanding, being cooperative and considerate have increasingly been replaced by more of an "instant pudding," "instant gratification," "It's really all about me," "I want it now," "Move over or I will run you over," "I'm not going to wait in line" spirit, tone, and approach to life.

During my lifetime, I've seen a dramatic shift from community to the individual, and unfortunately, I think, to more of an "anything and everything goes" mentality and behavior. Maybe it's my age, and maybe it's just generational. But, from my experience, running and financial-investment performance improve when there's consistency and commitment over time. Shortcuts, quick fixes, and "instant-pudding results" aren't usually part of long-term running or investment success. I've found that being dedicated and consistent usually generates positive returns in both running and investing, and I think we should be in both for the long haul.

My Story on Running

by John MacDonald

Running is my one-stop shop for health. Every facet of my living being has benefited from running. I have been running since high school. I started by running track, and then continued with thirty-two years in the US Army at various running distances. I have run full marathons, half marathons, 10Ks, 5Ks, triathlons, and trail runs all across the United States!

I can tell you firsthand that no other activity has helped me regulate my well-being better than running. Besides rewarding me with better health, running has given me the ability to see and smell every nuance of nature and urban nooks throughout this great country, from Maine to California. And, because of this, I am in a constant state of "runner's high," longing to hit another street or trail and plan my next run.

Photo of John MacDonald at 2018 Mount Rushmore Half Marathon
(Photo courtesy of retired Colonel MacDonald, US Army)

A "surprise encounter" during a run near Mount Rushmore (Photo courtesy of retired Colonel John MacDonald, US Army)

RUNNING COMPETITION

Running competition is a topic that probably means different things to different runners. There's competition among and between runners, and it pretty much occurs at all levels, with maybe the most intense competition taking place at Olympic Games or when stakes are highest at some of the more prestigious running events. That's not to say there isn't important competition at local community running events. There certainly is, and it's rewarding to win or place in smaller races and bring a trophy or special medal home after a good, honest effort!

Running and running competition are about time. It's about getting from the start to finish faster than other runners. But, I think it's also the way runners measure themselves. That is, I think the internal dimension of competition reveals inner effort, heart, determination, speed, and stamina. In each and every race, runners can gauge their inner effort and running effectiveness, and honestly measure what they did and how well they did it. The clock may tell the time, but more importantly, I think what happens inside the runner is the true measure and story of running competition.

In every race, runners are in touch with their inner selves. There is an ongoing internal self-monitoring, and runners measure their own mental, physical, and emotional readiness, capability, toughness, and how they respond to, meet, and overcome the known and unpredictable race challenges encountered from the start to the finish line.

In the end, runners know whether or not they gave it their all. They know whether or not their training and other race preparations were enough, more than enough, or if they fell short. Maybe somewhere in that "inner truth" runners find the true meaning of competition.

> *"True happiness involves the full use of one's power and talents."*
>
> **—John W. Gardner**

THE RUNNER INSIDE

"The way to get started is to quit talking and begin doing."

— **Walt Disney**

Watching athletic performance can be fun. I guess it could be called "spectating," or looking at what athletes and teams do from the outside, from the spectator's point of view. Spectators see the action and the result. They have an "outer view" and enjoy watching someone else do something. Whether it's watching a baseball player hit a home run, or make an amazing defensive play, or pitch a terrific game, it's often exciting to see.

Spectators pack football and soccer stadiums, fill arenas to watch basketball and ice hockey, and so on. Spectators line golf-course fairways just to see their favorite golfers hit shots. Spectators line roads and pack bleachers at major marathon races, and it is incredibly exciting just to get a glimpse of lead runners as they fly by in pursuit of the lead and finish line! Spectators see the runners' bodies moving forward, runners' arms and legs working in unison as they continue their herculean efforts to conquer the 26.2-mile distance.

In contrast, some sprint-distance races can be over in a flash—a mere nine, ten, twenty seconds up to one minute often constitute the extent of the race—but it is undeniably an exciting and even electric experience watching runners move at full speed, all out from start to finish.

But, I think the real story isn't in what we see the athletes do; it's instead in what we don't see. It's what's happening inside the athletes during their performance. Athletes know performance decisions are often made in split seconds. They don't have the luxury of seeing themselves performing. In their mind's eye, they see the track, road, or field. They see competitors and maybe the clock, but that's the extent of it. The decisions athletes make in the heat of competition are made proactively, reactively, and they can sometimes be a combination of both. Decisions concerning what to do and what not to do reflect an internal goal or objective, and multifaceted stream and blend of athletic, situational intelligence, experience, courage, determination, insight, and intuition.

The internal process athletes experience in the heat of competition can never be seen or fully appreciated by spectators. Athlete spectators may have a fuller, richer understanding of what they are seeing, because maybe, to some extent, they've performed in the sport themselves.

Yes, what runners, especially distance runners, think and feel during their competitions can best be understood by fellow distance runners. The gliding and grinding by distance runners through each mile, mile after mile, can best be appreciated by others who have done it, too. Nonrunner spectators can only imagine what it is like and can never ever really understand what a marathoner experiences.

Yes, I think the meaning of the run, the story of the run, the process of the run can truly be understood from the place and perspective of the runner inside.

"In time, you will discover running isn't just what you do; it's who you are."
— **Richard C. Goodwin**

THE RUNNER ESCAPE

"In need of a getaway or vacation? Take a long run on a scenic trail."

— Richard C. Goodwin

Is running a form of escape? Is running an activity and a time through which we can leave our problems behind and instead enter a problem-free zone and friendlier place? Maybe it is. At least for an hour or so, we can chug along, have an opportunity to find our inner selves, and settle into whatever world and space we want or need. It can be therapeutic, relaxing, and undeniably a healthy activity and time well spent. It can be time spent away from the grind of daily life and all the problems life sometimes presents.

But, is it actually an escape?

After the run, we find ourselves right back at it again with all our problems front and center, don't we? But, are those problem situations the same, or have they somehow changed as a result of running? Maybe running has energized us, given us added stamina, energy, increased optimism, and a renewed capacity for problem solving. Maybe it's helped bolster our ability to cope, and maybe it's helped provide us with the added resolve we've needed.

Maybe running isn't really an escape at all! Maybe running shuttles us off into a time and place of sanctuary, insight, faith, and healing, where we can discover the tools and solutions we seek to move forward with renewed spirit, determination, and passion for life.

> *"There is nothing so terrible as activity without insight."*
>
> **—Johann Wolfgang von Goethe**

Photo of a Cape Cod Rail Trial (CCRT) section near Brewster, Cape Cod

Remembering a Run and Visit with Mom

by Tom Warren

Thinking back to high school—well, at least at *my* high school—the coaches for various sports would recruit you to try out for their team/sport. First, as a junior, I tried out for basketball. At only five feet eleven inches, I was the second-tallest kid (and I failed to mention I was a band geek—first trumpet, first chair!), and that basketball experience turned out to be just so-so. Anyway, here is my running story.

I guess I have always been a runner. Lace 'em up and go! In 2002, at the young age of forty-eight (just kidding!), I was introduced to the Cape Cod Athletic Club. That's where I ran some of their various events and they extended a special invite for me to run the Boston Marathon. Just shy of fifty, this was something that was on my bucket list. At any rate, I accepted the invitation and trained six hundred miles in seventeen weeks through blizzards, freezing winds, sleet, and all the fun stuff to get ready to go.

In 2003, at the one hundred and seventh running of the Boston Marathon, I was at the starting line and ready for the race to begin! I finished under four hours in a time of 3:49.

My mom, an eighty-four-year-old former teacher, was in an assisted-living facility at the time of the race, and when I walked in to visit her with my Boston Marathon jacket and medal the following Tuesday, she was sitting in the dining room along with many other elders. She was all smiles to see me. When I walked in, the elders stood up and cheered! Mom and I could not have been more proud, and I was especially happy for her.

Sometimes, it's not about the run; it's about the result and what happens after the run is over. God bless you, Mom (she is now deceased)!

I have run with the great Johnny Kelley many times, the Hoyts, and many others over the years, but I will cherish this memory of the Boston Marathon and my visit with Mom most of all.

Photo of Tom Warren and the author, 2018, at the Johnny Kelley Memorial and Park, Dennis, Cape Cod

Running through My Life

by Margaret Marcinkowski

I remember the first time I ever ran any significant distance. I was eight years old and had been at a school fair. I had used all of my money to play arcade games. So, I ran home to get more money out of my piggy bank. We lived exactly one half of a mile from my school. I remember thinking I needed to get my money and get back before the good prizes were gone. I ran home and ran back without stopping either direction. I was very proud of myself. I recall bragging to my mother that I ran the entire way home and back. One whole mile! My mother was not as thrilled as I was. I had not told her where I had gone.

In the 1970s, Title IX was passed. Title IX was a federal law that essentially prohibited educational institutions from discriminatory differential treatment of women. As a girl attending high school beginning in 1975, Title IX effectively ensured girls would be able to play organized varsity sports in high school. As a result of Title IX, my high school was actively recruiting girls to participate in varsity sports. It was probably a less competitive time to be able to participate on a varsity sports team, but it was also a lot of fun. We had uniforms, rides to competitions, and a coach to train us.

It likely seems shocking to girls today, but my high school did not have girls' varsity sports teams prior to Title IX, and many people were not supportive of girls' participation in sports, either.

Once, when I was at a high school track, I told my father I would show him how to run over a hurdle. A woman sitting nearby in the stadium overheard me talking to my dad. She smiled and told me not to run on the track over a hurdle because it was not lady-like. My mother, standing right by me, immediately told me to go out there and do it! It was a very uncomfortable moment. I did not want people to think I was not ladylike, but I really enjoyed running. My parents, who were divorced and really did not agree on much, both insisted I should ignore people who talked like that. My parents both were adamant that their daughters would not be treated differently than their sons. And, people who disagreed were wrong. I was extraordinarily fortunate that my parents both encouraged all their children to participate in and enjoy sports, especially running.

I went to high school, and it was there I started running for sport. A friend convinced me to join the girls' track team, and that is where my love for running truly began.

After joining the track team, I soon learned that I was not a sprinter. I preferred the one- and two-mile races, and I found that I enjoyed the whole running experience. I was never the fastest. I never won a blue ribbon. I never made it to the state track competition, but I never stopped running and competing. I went to college and running became my exercise, my stress reducer, my method of clearing my mind, and part of who I was.

As I got older, I had children, a few small injuries, and had to take breaks from running. Invariably, I would be happy when I was able to run again. But, my biggest running gap occurred when I was thirty-six years old. I was diagnosed with acute myelogenous leukemia. I knew I had not felt up to a run for a couple of weeks, but could not believe I was that sick.

Yet, I was. I was treated with multiple rounds of chemotherapy and an allogeneic bone-marrow transplant. My brother was my donor. During the treatment, I walked each day around the hospital's bone marrow transplant unit for exercise. Afterwards, I would stare out the hospital window and watch runners jog by the hospital. It truly broke my soul. I felt devastated that I was so sick, and was not certain I would survive. I knew that I might never run again. It was a particularly difficult feeling to think I may have already gone on my last run in my life.

One day, while sitting by the window in my hospital room, my brother came in to visit me. He told me he had a dream the night before. In it, he saw me running in the rain with my three children, and he said I was healthy and happy! This was, honestly, the most spectacular and encouraging thing anyone said to me during this ordeal. This image made me so completely happy, and I thought of it often.

I did survive leukemia. Only six months after completing my treatment, I signed up with my brother to participate in a 10K run to raise money for leukemia research. I could not even run one mile, but I was in the race and participating. My brother ran and walked with me, and we finished behind the trucks that were collecting the cones. I was so happy to complete the 10K race and get an official time. That day was wonderful!

It has now been almost twenty years since I was sick, and I continue to run. I have run in the rain. I have run with my children. I have run with my husband (who has now learned to enjoy running also). I have run with my brother and sister. I have run half marathons, 10Ks, 5Ks, ten milers, five milers, and I even have "run" (honestly, a lot of starting and stopping after mile twenty) a full marathon.

I cannot imagine my life without running, and I am happy to report that I finally have won a medal! I came in third place in my division in my town's 5K Turkey Trot! I am very proud of that medal.

Photo of Margaret Marcinkowski and her daughter, Annie (Photo courtesy of Margaret Marcinkowski)

"Believe you can and you're halfway there."
—Theodore Roosevelt

Time to Reset?

One of the things I've always liked about year-end is it provides a certain finality for that year's activities. It provides an occasion to review what's been accomplished, what's gone wrong, how things have progressed, what needs to be done, and of course, I can also recount the many reasons to be grateful one last time before the New Year kicks in. I usually try to slow down, and it's a time when my focus changes. And, for many in the community of runners, it can be a time to complete an inventory of training logs, miles run, injuries sustained, races completed, awards won, and so on.

At year-end, that year's chapter on running is closed and a new chapter is about to be experienced, written, and read. In other words, it can serve as a time for a much-needed running reset. For instance, just because the year was dedicated to long-distance training and races doesn't necessarily mean the same running goals and objectives should hold true in the New Year. Instead, maybe the New Year "reset" can point to shorter-distance training and races. Maybe it will provide for a blend of both short- and long-distance training and race opportunities. Maybe the New Year reset will include a pathway for running differently. Running differently in the New Year may provide exciting and new running pleasure, as well as a well-earned refresher.

Running "stale" can become tedious, humdrum running. Consequently, repeating the same running program year-in and

year-out could interfere with running enjoyment and exuber-
ance. Further, a running "reset" isn't required to be just one
time—say, at year-end—but it can also take place whenever it's
necessary or seemingly the "right" time to try one.

All it really takes is to push the "reset" button and then run
forward again from there!

*"Vitality shows in not only the ability to persist but
the ability to start over."*

—**F. Scott Fitzgerald**

SUPERMAN

It was the 1950s, and I remember growing up with Superman! I seem to remember playing Superman in my living room. I recall running, and then launching my body out into the air, and then landing onto the living-room couch when I was age six or seven. I remember turning one of my small blankets into a makeshift Superman cape. I thought wearing my Superman cape gave me extra superpower, and it would help me fly across the room! I had Superman comics, watched Superman on TV (Superman was then played by the late George Reeves), and could sing the *Superman* TV show songs. Superman was "faster than a speeding bullet, more powerful than a locomotive, able to leap tall buildings in a single bound." He was amazing!

Several years ago, at age sixty-six, I was running down a neighboring sidewalk. I was in marathon training at the time, and it was a very hot, sunny day, and I was finishing my fourth two-mile loop. I was tired, and didn't realize I was shuffling more and not lifting my feet with each stride forward like I normally would. And, I wasn't paying close attention to the pavement and sidewalk cracks. I was thinking of something else when suddenly my left toe hit against a raised portion of sidewalk, causing me to fall and slide forward onto my face and front. It hurt, and I was stunned!

After I got up off the ground and checked myself out, I discovered my knees, face, hands, and arms were scraped and bloodied.

From what I could initially tell, the fall hadn't resulted in more serious injuries, and after I regained my senses, stood, and walked a bit, I decided to jog the remaining short distance back home to tend to my superficial wounds. I said to myself, "What a dope you are! How could you have fallen like that? You know better than to do something like that. You're *so lucky* you didn't *really* hurt yourself!" I also made a self-commitment to *never fall like that again!*

The following weekend, I visited a nearby running store to share my story with one of the salesmen. After hearing my tale of woe, he said, "You did a Superman!" Then he said, "I bet that really hurt!"

I'd never heard that expression before, so I asked him what he meant. He explained when I fell forward onto my front and face with arms and hands extended out, I had actually "done a Superman." I thought about what he said, finally understood it, and I told him that was the first and last time I'd ever "do a Superman" fall along a sidewalk, or anywhere else again!

I learned a valuable lesson. Even though I was running a familiar route, I still needed to stay alert and maintain good, solid running form. I didn't, and consequently I paid a price for it. Fortunately, I didn't sustain more serious injuries from the fall. And, as much as I like the Superman character portrayed in books, movies, and on TV, I'm resolved to never "do a Superman" sidewalk fall again!

(*Superman* is credited to creators and writer Jerry Siegel and illustrator Joe Shuster, DC Comics, and the syndicated TV show *Adventures of Superman*, which originally appeared from 1952–1958.)

"Even if you fall on your face, you're still moving forward."

—Victor Kiam

IT NEVER ENDS

Remember your first visit to a running store, talking to someone about getting started in running, getting fitted for and then trying on your first pair of running shoes, buying the shoes, running in the shoes for the first time, and experiencing your first run? It was as though everything was in front of you back then. And remember how, over time, you got into shape, decided on your first race, and completed your first race? Remember that feeling of excitement and accomplishment? And remember running through those initial days, weeks, and then months and becoming a consistent runner? Do you remember when you discovered running had become an integral part of your life? Remember when you decided to try running your first half-marathon race? And, do you remember when you set your sights on the 26.2-mile distance, trained for it, and completed it? Do you remember all the training you did, all the miles you logged, and all the sacrifice you made to reach those milestones? Do you remember the time and place you realized you had become a *runner*?

Running provides new growth opportunities and life insight as we continue to run consistently over time. And, no matter how many years we run, no matter what our pace, and no matter how many finish lines we cross, I believe running will always provide us with new and rich experiences, regardless of our age.

It really never ends.

"Running isn't just about finding yourself. Running is about creating yourself."

—Richard C. Goodwin

LOCK 32 CANAL PARK AND ERIE CANAL

I've found one of the most beautiful places to run is on the running pathway alongside the Erie Canal in Pittsford, New York. As I run up and down the pathway, I especially enjoy watching boats traveling alongside me on the canal waters. There's activity all around: people walking and talking, people riding their bicycles, kids feeding ducks that congregate near the shore, Erie Canal sightseeing boat tours departing from neighboring docks, and of course, there's the two-mile run to nearby Lock 32.

When I arrive to the lock, I stop and wait to see if a boat is approaching. If a boat approaches, I know I will soon see the lock in operation. I never get tired of watching Lock 32 work, seeing water levels rise and fall, and then watching boats come through the lock safely on their passages up and down the waterway.

During my most recent visit and run to Lock 32, I came upon a family of four that was eager to see a boat come through. I talked to them briefly and mentioned I had first come to Lock 32 on a school trip when I was in first grade, back in the mid-1950s. Had it really been over sixty years ago?

I am grateful to have spent some time with that very nice family and to have had the opportunity to observe the two wide-eyed children look up and down the canal with anticipation, hoping they would soon see a boat arrive.

The next day, I shared the run to Lock 32 with my thirty-year-old son. It was a beautiful day and a terrific shared experience. The Erie Canal, the running pathway, the beautiful scenery, and Lock 32 didn't disappoint.

Oh, about those two children—a boat *did* arrive in about ten minutes, and the kids *did* see Lock 32 in operation, and I doubt they will ever forget it!

Photo of the Pittsford, New York, area Erie Canalway Trail, ideal for biking, walking, and running

Photo of the Erie Canal "Lock E32" in Pittsford, New York

Photo of the author's son, Rich Jr., at the Erie Canal Lock 32, Pittsford, New York, site

RUNNING FREE

Let's face it: Most of the time we're running, we are training for something—some race somewhere—and with a goal and finishing time in mind. Goals, objectives, and race plans are important and an integral part of our running experience.

But, every so often we find ourselves as runners in life and running situations that somehow pry us out of the daily grind and runner commitments we find ourselves in. It could be a running injury that has sidelined us over an extended period of time. It could be our time and energy are needed elsewhere. Or, it could just be we've reached a stage in our running careers and process where we suddenly discover the pure joy of running—no strings attached! I like to think of it as the "self-actualization" of runners. It truly is running without some predetermined reason or purpose. It's running with nothing particular in mind other than enjoying the experience of running and remaining open to how running truly feels. It's finding that state of mind, heart, and body where and when nothing else matters or is thought of during the run. It's the awareness of all the senses being joined and wrapped around, in, and through whatever the run brings us. We become the run, and the run becomes us.

I like to think of it as running free.

Run-4 Miles-for Life

I've discovered, on average, running four miles—or spending approximately thirty-five to forty-five minutes per run—four or five times weekly over many months and years has helped me establish and maintain a pretty decent level of fitness. Of course, I've varied my weekly mileage over the years depending on what my training objectives and race goals have been, but I've come to believe the four miles, four or five times a week, is the key to keeping a higher fitness level and maintaining a sense of emotional well-being, as well as a positive mindset.

I've discussed this with my runner friends, and to my surprise, they've told me they follow similar patterns of miles per run and number of runs per week when they are trying to maintain their running and fitness levels. I realize it's all adjustable and situational per runner, and for some runners the mileage and runs per week may be too much, and for others, not enough. It all depends!

But, I do believe the phrase and concept I've coined ("run-4 miles-for life") provides a simple, compact, and straightforward formula for running effectiveness, life quality, and maybe even longevity, if followed consistently over time.

The great, accomplished, and legendary runner Bill Rodgers once ended a note to me with the following: "Let's run forever!" Maybe that's the ultimate, lifelong runner goal, dream, and lasting reward for those of us who have been true lifelong runners. I guess only time will tell.

SOME FINAL THOUGHTS

Again, writing this book has truly been a labor of love. I've learned that we, as lifelong runners and members of the running community, have lots in common. And, it may be our essential common denominator and one shared trait: we are all strivers. I think that's absolutely true for the lifelong runners I've known, and it describes the contributors to this book.

The term "strivers" came to me well after I'd finished writing this book, after I'd had some time to reflect a bit. I think "striver" fits, because that's what we all do! We strive when we run day in and day out, year after year.

What does it mean to strive? Dictionary definitions include the terms "to compete," "to struggle." My experience has revealed lifelong runners do these things: they exert themselves, they are vigorous and try hard, they contend, compete, and accept running challenges, and they embrace the struggle. They are consistent in their training, and they are not quitters. They are strivers. We are strivers, and I believe being strivers is what keeps us going and ultimately transforms us into lifelong runners.

Once again, I want to thank my wife, Judy, and son, Rich, for being part of my lifelong running journey, and also recognize and give special thanks to each of my very accomplished friends, colleagues, and special book contributors for sharing their journeys, stories, and insights about running. They are Tony Cianciola, Cara Reilly, Beth Whitehurst, John MacDonald, Geoff Martin, Lindsay Billings, Sunjune Lee, Kent Scriber, Tom Warren, Margaret Marcinkowski, and the great Bill Rodgers.

And, I want to extend very special thanks to all the many amazing pioneers of running who blazed trails for us and who have provided—and continue to provide—life-lasting inspiration.

Lastly, I want recognize *you*—all my fellow veteran, lifelong runners. May each of you continue your running . . . forever!

"You just can't beat the person who never gives up."
—**Babe Ruth**

Dedication and Special Acknowledgments

Thanks for the amazing running events and to the many race organizers and numerous volunteers that have provided me, the book contributors, and many other lifelong runners with so many wonderful running experiences.

In particular, thanks to:

1. The New York City Marathon (and its various major sponsors over the years) and the New York Road Runners club
2. The Boston Marathon and the Boston Athletic Association
3. The Falmouth Road Race and the Falmouth Road Race, Inc.
4. The Long Island Marathon
5. The Cape Cod Marathon and Marathon Half, and the Cape Cod Athletic Club
6. The Kiawah Island Marathon and Half Marathon
7. The Rocket City Marathon
8. The Chickamauga Battlefield Marathon
9. The Walt Disney World Marathon
10. The Jacksonville Marathon
11. The Atlanta Marathon
12. The Publix-Georgia Marathon and Half Marathon, and the Atlanta Track Club
13. The Ironman-KONA
14. The AJC Peachtree Road Race and the Atlanta Track Club

Special thanks to legendary runners and running contributors Bill Rodgers, Joan Benoit Samuelson, Frank Shorter, Jeff Galloway, Hal Higdon, Eamonn Coghlan, Dean Karnazes, Dave McGillivray, and the late greats Jim Fixx, Johnny Kelley, Ted Corbitt, Fred Lebow, Dr. George Sheehan, Dr. Norbert Sander, and Grete Waitz, among many others, for all they've given to the sport of running, and for inspiring each of us in the running community.

MEET THE CONTRIBUTORS

Geoff Martin, PhD: Geoff is retired from Consumers Union, a former college teacher, former marathoner, and Boston Marathon qualifier.

Kent Scriber, PhD: Professor emeritus at Ithaca College, author, member of state and national athletic-trainer halls of fame and the Ithaca College Athletics Hall of Fame. Kent is a multiple marathoner.

Tony Cianciola: Tony is a teacher, coach, and department chair, high school (HS) health and physical education, certified trainer, an accomplished marathoner, Boston Marathon qualifier, and triathlete.

Cara Reilly: Cara is a HS counselor, coach, and she excels at running all distances. She is a multiple-time Boston Marathon finisher.

Sunjune Lee: Sunjune is an ESOL HS teacher, and she has completed twenty full marathons, including the Boston Marathon.

Tom Warren: Tom manages the Brewster Green Resort in Cape Cod and has completed numerous races, including the Boston Marathon.

Margaret Marcinkowski: Margaret is an attorney and specialist in technology. She has completed multiple races, including half marathons and a full marathon. Margaret is a cancer survivor.

Elizabeth Whitehurst: Beth is a HS educator, and she has completed multiple 5K, 10K, and half-marathon races. Her husband, David, and son, Charlie, are former NFL quarterbacks.

Lindsay Billings: Lindsay is an ACC academic honor-roll cross-country runner for Duke University and past recipient of numerous HS running awards.

John MacDonald, PhD: John is a HS teacher and coach, a

retired colonel of the US Army, Bronze Star recipient, triathlete, and marathoner.

Bill Rodgers: The great and legendary American runner who has inspired so many of us in the worldwide runner community.

ABOUT THE AUTHOR

Richard Goodwin Sr. is a lifelong runner, having completed numerous races from 5K to full-marathon distances over the past forty years. He is a Vietnam-era army veteran, retired high school teacher, retired banker and insurance executive, former businessman, financial planner, and university assistant professor and adjunct professor of business, management, and economics.

Rich played three sports in high school and Division I and II baseball at Ithaca College, where he received a BA in economics. He subsequently earned an MBA from the University of Connecticut. In 2018, his former 1967 American Legion State Championship baseball team was recognized as "the Team of the Ages," and was inducted into the Rochester, New York, Frontier Field Walk of Fame.